THE 8 HABITS OF MENTAL TOUGHNESS

CRACK THE MINDSET FOR THRIVING UNDER PRESSURE, CONQUER ANY CHALLENGE AND BECOME UNSTOPPABLE

WISDOM UNIVERSITY

CONTENTS

THE BULLETPROOF MIND

10 MENTORS OF MENTAL TOUGHNESS

Your 60 Second Review Can Change Everything For Us

Whether you've just picked up this book or have already started reading, we'd love it if you could take just 1 minute to leave a quick review. It's as easy as scanning the QR code or following the short link below.

Your feedback—whether it's about the book's topic or your excitement to dive in—is incredibly important for us. Reviews not only offer us valuable feedback, but they also play a big role in shaping how this book reaches a broader audience.

If you'd like to go the extra mile, consider attaching a photo of the book—whether it's the cover or a glimpse of the content—making your review stand out to other readers.

Your review, even with just a few words and a quick photo, makes a world of difference. Thank you for being a part of this journey!

Christoph M.   *Michael M.*

Founders of Wisdom University

Go to: t.ly/t8homtr

Get ALL our upcoming eBooks for FREE
(Yes, you've read that right)
Total Value: $199.80*

You'll get exclusive access to our books before they hit the online shelves and enjoy them for free.

Additionally, you'll receive the following bonuses:

Bonus Nr. 1
Our Bestseller
How To Start Mind Mapping
Total Value: $9.99

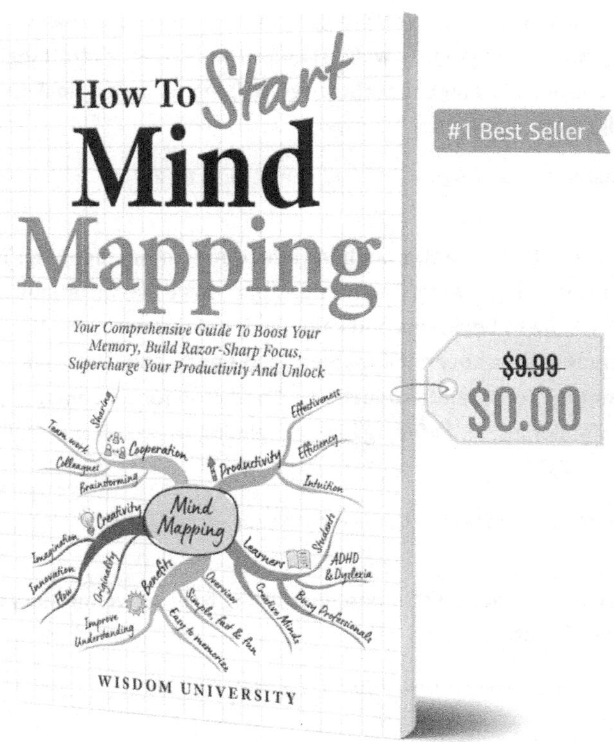

Do you ever feel like your brain is overloaded?

Like there's too much information swirling around and you can't keep track of it all?

Introducing mind mapping – a powerful tool that lets you visualize your thoughts!

This book is packed with step-by-step guides that show you exactly how to create mind-blowing mind maps for any subject or task.

"This book is an excellent resource for anyone interested in improving their cognitive skills and boosting productivity through mind mapping. It offers clear, step-by-step instructions on how to get started with mind mapping, making it accessible even for beginners. The guide is well-organized and covers everything from the basics to advanced techniques, helping readers unlock their full creative potential."

HK007 - Reviewed in the United States on August 12, 2024

"The book offers a thorough introduction to mind mapping. There are clear, step-by-step instructions that make the technique accessible to beginners and valuable for seasoned users. It demonstrates how mind mapping can significantly improve memory, focus, and productivity. Good read for students, professionals, and lifelong learners aiming to unlock their full potential."

Passionate - Reviewed in the United States on August 7, 2024

"This is a great book for people wanting to improve memory and cognitive abilities!"

Lisa - Reviewed in the United States on August 12, 2024

"This book is your ticket to turning chaos into creativity. Perfect for students, professionals, or anyone looking to upgrade their mental toolkit, 'How To Start Mind Mapping' will teach you how to map your way to brilliance. With scientific backing and real-world success stories, this isn't just another productivity hack — it's a mental game-changer. Cannot wait to put it to practice!"

@Msrexti - Reviewed in the United States on August 16, 2024

Bonus Nr. 2

Our Bestseller
The Art Of Game Theory
Total Value: $9.99

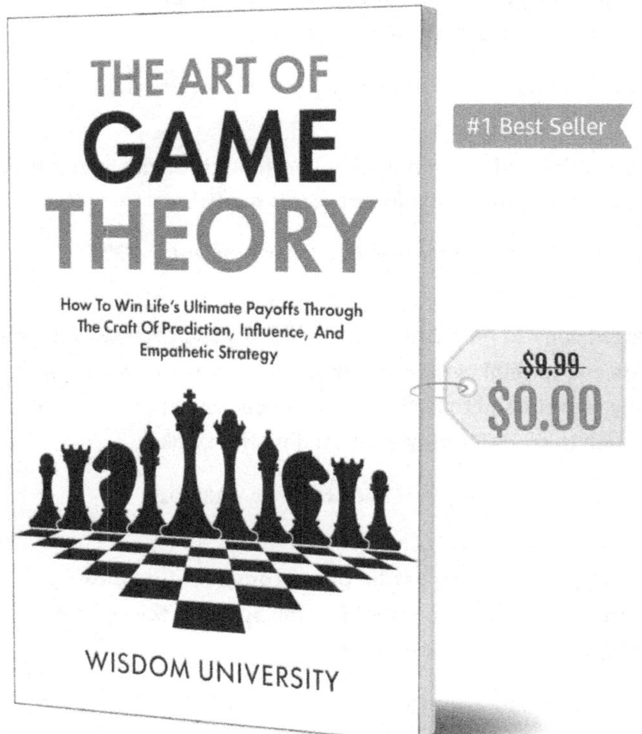

Step into the fascinating world of game theory with *The Art Of Game Theory*!

This expertly written book for beginners will introduce you to strategic decision-making and show you how game theory applies to diverse fields in clear and simple terms.

Whether you're a student, professional, or lifelong learner, *The Art Of Game Theory* equips you with powerful tools to gain a strategic edge in life.

"Thanks Wisdom University! This book offers simple strategies one can use to achieve things in your personal life. Anyone of average intelligence can read, understand and be in a position to enact the suggestions contained within."

David L. Jones - Reviewed in the United States on November 12, 2023

"Haven't finished it yet, but what I've gone through so far is just incredible! Another great job from this publisher!"

W. S. Jones - Reviewed in the United States on October 12, 2023

"A great book to help you through difficult and complex problems. It gets you to think differently about what you are dealing with. Highly recommend to both new and experienced problem solvers. You with think differently after reading this book."

Thom - Reviewed in the United States on October 18, 2023

"I like this book and how it simplifies complex ideas into something to use in everyday life. I am applying the concept and gaining a lot of clarity and insight."

Ola - Reviewed in the United States on October 18, 2023

"The book is an excellent introduction to game theory. The writing is clear, and the analysis is first-rate. Concrete, real-world examples of theory are presented, and both the ways in which game theory effectively models what actually happens in life is cogently evaluated. I also appreciate the attention paid to the ethical dimensions of applying game theory in many situations."

Amazon Customer - Reviewed in the United States on October 8, 2023

Bonus Nr. 3 & 4

Thinking Sheets
Break Your Thinking Patterns
&
Flex Your Wisdom Muscle
Total Value Each: $4.99

<u>A glimpse into what you'll discover inside:</u>

- How to expose the sneaky flaws in your thinking and what it takes to fix them (the included solutions are dead-simple)
- Dozens of foolproof strategies to make sound and regret-free decisions leading you to a life of certainty and fulfillment
- How to elevate your rationality to extraordinary levels (this will put you on a level with Bill Gates, Elon Musk and Warren Buffett)
- Hidden gems of wisdom to guide your thoughts and actions (gathered from the smartest minds of all time)

Here's everything you get:

- ✔ How To Start Mind Mapping eBook   ($9.99 Value)
- ✔ The Art Of Game Theory eBook   ($9.99 Value)
- ✔ Break Your Thinking Patterns Sheet   ($4.99 Value)
- ✔ Flex Your Wisdom Muscle Sheet   ($4.99 Value)
- ✔ All our upcoming eBooks   ($199.80* Value)

Total Value: $229.76

Go to the end of the book for the offer!

*If you download 20 of our books for free, this would equal a value of 199.80$

WHAT READERS ARE SAYING ABOUT WISDOM UNIVERSITY

"Wisdom University embodies an innovative and progressive educational approach, expertly merging deep academic insights with contemporary learning techniques. Their books are not only insightful and captivating but also stand out for their emphasis on practical application, making them a valuable resource for both academic learning and real-world personal development."

—Bryan Kornele, 55 years old, Software Engineer from the United States

"Wisdom University teaches factual Management Techniques. I would recommend their books to any managers."

—Brett Gaskin, MSc in Physics, Senior Quality Manager in the high-tech industry

"I have been reading books from Wisdom University for a while now and have been impressed with the CONDENSED AND VALUABLE INFORMATION they contain. Reading these books allows me to LEARN

INFORMATION QUICKLY AND EASILY, so I can put the knowledge to practice right away to improve myself and my life. I recommend it for busy people who don't have a LOT of time to read, but want to learn: Wisdom University gives you the opportunity to easily and quickly learn a lot of useful, practical information, which helps you have a better, more productive, successful, and happier life. It takes the information and wisdom of many books and distills and organizes the most useful and helpful information down into a smaller book, so you spend more time applying helpful information, rather than reading volumes of repetition and un-needed filler text.

—Dawn Campo, Degree in Human psychology and Business, Office administrator from Utah

"I'm a subscriber of Wisdom University for over a year now. I would recommend Wisdom University books to anyone who wants to improve their understanding of cognitive behavioural therapeutic principles."

—Sunil Punjabi, Maharashtra (India), 52, PhD, Psychologist

"I wanted to read some books about thinking and learning which have some depth. I can say "Wisdom University" is one of the most valuable and genuine brands I have ever seen. Their books are top-notch at kindle. I have read their books on learning, thinking, etc.

& they are excellent. I would especially recommend their latest book "Think Like Da Vinci" to those who want to have brilliant & clear thinking."

"Wisdom University books are simple, direct, easy to read and focused on the topic. I would recommend them to people related to critical thinking, creative thinking, philosophy and social studies."

—Manuel Vazquez, PhD in International Relations, Principal Researcher

"I have most of the ebooks & audiobooks that Wisdom University has created. I prefer audiobooks as found on Audible. The people comprising Wisdom University do an excellent job of providing quality personal development materials. They offer value for everyone interested in self-improvement."

—Neal Cheney, double major in Computer-Science & Mathematics, retired 25yrs USN (Nuclear Submarines) and retired Computer Programmer

"I would recommend these books to my grandson."

—Daniel, Florida (USA), 69, Bachelor Degree, retired

INTRODUCTION

From Surviving To Thriving: How To Forge Your Mental Toughness With *The 8 Habits Of Mental Toughness*

Do you feel like life keeps getting harder, and you struggle to keep up? It can seem like life's obstacles get tougher and more frequent with each passing year. Constant stress, hardship, and difficulties can wear anyone down. If you find yourself just surviving rather than thriving in the face of life's difficulties, this mental toughness book bundle is for you.

Mental toughness is the mindset that makes challenges something to learn from, not something to fear. Resilience, adaptability, and the ability to view challenges as opportunities are key traits. Mentally tough individuals view the world around them through a different lens, one that exudes confidence in their abilities to grow to meet the demands of an increasingly fast-paced modern world. It is the secret ingredient to unleashing your hidden potential and achieving your wildest dreams.

And it is my hope that this two-book bundle will help you

learn the secrets of mental toughness and provide the inspiration you need.

The Bulletproof Mind will show you how to develop a mentally tough outlook on life that encompasses the habits and skills necessary to overcome even the toughest challenges and turn them into success. It provides a step-by-step blueprint to build mental toughness and how to use it to improve your life. Rather than feeling at the mercy of what life throws your way, you will build the tools to regain control and bounce back from setbacks stronger than before.

Need more inspiration to keep you motivated while you work on your mental toughness? *10 Mentors of Mental Toughness* brings you the stories of ten regular people who achieved incredible success in their chosen fields despite facing what appeared to be insurmountable obstacles. These men and women from different walks of life overcame incredible odds to succeed in sports, politics, business, philanthropy, and more. When the challenges you face seem overwhelming, find hope and direction in the stories of these ten individuals.

Living the principles of mental toughness has been a game-changer for me, and I'm proud to share what I have learned through this two-book bundle. Juggling my various roles—writer, editor, educator, parent-support advocate for children with disabilities, wife, mother, family member, and friend—requires managing stress, prioritizing how I use my time, and overcoming setbacks to keep moving forward. Living in three countries over ten years also required the strength and perseverance to make a new life with each new move. I had to learn to practice the 4 Cs of mental toughness to manage it without burning out.

Control: While no one can completely control their circumstances, I strive to control my reactions to life's obstacles. I analyze my emotions and then channel them in the best way possible, choosing the best response to a difficult scenario rather than allowing a temporary emotion to get in the way of the best solution.

Commitment: I commit to my goals through perseverance, dedication, and resilience. More than motivation, commitment keeps me going, even when I don't feel like it. It gets me across the finish line.

Challenge: Mentally tough people approach obstacles as challenges, and I do too. It's about perception. It isn't about toxic positivity—it's recognizing that some challenges are life-changing. It is about choosing how to best move forward despite the circumstances.

Confidence: Mentally tough individuals are confident in handling what life throws them. They know they can learn the skill, ask for help, and face life's challenges. Confidence was the most difficult for me to develop, and I still struggle occasionally, but I am confident I will continue to improve!

If you want to learn more about the 4Cs and how they and other mental toughness habits can improve your life, you've come to the right place. This bundle includes relatable anecdotes, strategies backed by research, action items, and inspiration from the 10 mentors to keep you on track.

If you're ready to commit and put in the work, I'm excited to see where this journey takes you.

Kathleen Sperduti

THE BULLETPROOF MIND

SHARPEN YOUR WITS, GET BACK ON YOUR FEET, AND THRIVE IN AN EVER-CHANGING WORLD

1

———

FROM SETBACKS TO SUCCESS

HOW MENTAL TOUGHNESS PLAYS A ROLE IN
YOUR TRIUMPH

Four-time NBA champion. Four-time NBA Finals MVP. Four-time NBA MVP. Sixteen-time NBA All-Star. NBA All-time lead scorer. LeBron James is a household name, a basketball icon, and one of the most decorated athletes in the history of the sport. And he defied the odds to get there.[1]

Born to an unwed, 16-year-old teenage mother in a poor part of Akron, Ohio, stardom was probably the last thing people expected of a young LeBron James. An absent father put the responsibility for raising him on his young mother. LeBron James' childhood was not easy. He and his mother struggled with poverty, moving several times when he was young, sometimes living with family, other times in shelters. Instability and uncertainty were constant forces in his life.

None of that stopped him.

Young LeBron showed promise as a basketball player from a young age. With the love of his mother and the dedication of his coach, he developed those early skills into something spectacular. He dedicated himself to the sport and put in the hard work and perseverance required to consistently improve his game. He saw the challenges facing him as opportunities to move forward, including ignoring the naysayers and moving to the NBA directly from high school instead of playing college ball.[2]

Over the years, he has shown a remarkable ability to keep calm under pressure, rise to every challenge, and commit to personal improvement every season. He is the epitome of a mentally tough individual.

We've all heard stories of famous athletes with difficult childhoods, injuries, or other setbacks who defy the odds and become the best at what they do. We are told that through hard work and dedication, they were able to overcome the obstacles in their path and rise to the top of their game.

But how? Every athlete works hard. Many athletes facing similar challenges never reach those levels of success. Some give up entirely before their careers ever really begin. What trait do successful athletes have that others don't?

Mental toughness.

It helps athletes push through rejection and failure, hardships, and most obstacles put in their path to become stronger, more resilient, and ultimately, more successful.

You might be asking, *So, how does this apply to me? I'm not an athlete looking to make it in the big leagues. I just want to be able to handle life's pressures and break out of this rut that's holding me back.*

That's the best part.

Mental toughness is not a trait specific to athletes and is not something you're born with. It's something anyone can learn. Mental toughness is an approach to living that can lead to success in all areas of life. More than hard work, more than dedication, and more than just being resilient, mental toughness embodies elements of all of these and more. And it can help you too.

Are you interested in learning how to level up at work, be more present at home, and have more fun in your free time? Let's get started!

Start with the 4 Cs

What exactly is mental toughness? Mental toughness is part mindset and part daily practice to increase one's ability to overcome challenges, manage stress and emotions effectively, and face life with a positive outlook. It combines cognitive, emotional, and behavioral skills to create a unique approach to life's challenges. Mental toughness is often described as being able to master the four Cs: Control, Commitment, Challenge, and Confidence.[3]

Control: While no one can completely control their circumstances, mentally tough individuals strive to control their reactions to life's obstacles. Mastering control over your emotions means that you choose the response to a difficult scenario rather than allowing a temporary emotion to get in the way of the best solution. Does that mean that mentally strong people ignore their feelings? Absolutely not! In fact, it's quite the opposite. Mentally tough people analyze their emotions and then channel those emotions constructively to control their response rather than letting their emotions control them.

Born in Pakistan in 1997, Malala Yousafzai's life changed when the Taliban took over her small village in 2008, forbidding girls to attend school. Malala spent the next few years of her life as an education activist, spreading the word about the importance of education for girls in her country.

And that made her a target.

In 2012, a gunman boarded her school bus, asked for her by name, and shot her in the head. She was flown to England for life-saving treatment and spent almost all of the following two years undergoing surgeries and various therapies to help her heal.

Following her recovery and newly established life in England, she was faced with a choice. Live a safe, quiet life in England, or continue her fight for education equality for girls in her home country of Pakistan and around the world. She chose the latter, deciding to take one of the most difficult situations anyone could ever face, and turn it into her life's mission to ensure that other girls would not become targets as well for pursuing an education.

She created the Malala Fund in 2014, dedicated to fighting for the rights of girls around the world to have equal access to education. She also received the Nobel Peace Prize in 2014, becoming the youngest-ever Nobel laureate. Malala took control of her life's circumstances and turned something extremely traumatic and negative into an inspiration for others worldwide.[4]

Commitment: Being committed to achieving goals is a key element of mental toughness. Commitment is different from motivation or having good intentions. Good intentions are great for goal setting. Motivation is what gets you started. Commitment in the form of perseverance, dedication, and resilience keeps you going, even when you don't feel like it or when life throws you curveballs. It is what gets you across the finish line.

Roger Federer, one of the greatest tennis players in the history of the game, was known for his commitment both on the court and off. He won 103 Association of Tennis Professionals (ATP) championship titles, and spent a record 302 weeks as the number-one player in the world. He retired holding the record for most Grand Slam men's singles championships, winning 20. At the time of his retirement, he held the men's singles record for most Wimbledon titles in the Open era, winning eight.

So, it might be surprising to learn that his Wimbledon experience didn't start so successfully. After winning the tournament as a junior in 1998, he struggled to find success there once he turned professional. In fact, he lost in the first round of the tournament the first three years he played it, and wasn't able to win his first Wimbledon title until 2003.

What changed?

As a junior player, he was known to be temperamental at times. Mastering his emotional control during matches after turning professional proved to be one of the keys to his long-term success, but his commitment to constantly improving his ability to adapt to any surface and any style of play really made the difference. Rather than letting those early losses discourage him, he rose to the challenge and committed to doing the work needed to succeed.[5]

Challenge: This is all about perception and general outlook on life. Do you perceive challenges as unfair? Inconvenient? Demoralizing? Or do you see them as opportunities to learn and grow? Thanks to a generally positive, optimistic outlook and a growth mindset, mentally tough people see challenges as opportunities and are excited to meet them headfirst. In the workforce, these are the problem solvers.

Most people would consider loss of limb a valid reason to quit a sport. But Bethany Hamilton is not like most people. Growing up dreaming of becoming a professional surfer, her dream was derailed one sunny morning in the waters off Hawai'i. In 2003, Bethany, 13 years old, went surfing with a friend and her father. Everything changed when Bethany was attacked by a 14-foot tiger shark while surfing, losing her left arm in the process.

The trauma of the attack, the struggle to physically recover, and the fear of getting back in the water would have been too many challenges for many to overcome. But Bethany never wavered in her commitment to recovery and to her dream of being a professional surfer. Incredibly, she returned to surfing just 26 days following the shark attack.

She won her first national championship two years later and was inducted into the Surfer's Hall of Fame in 2017. She continues to surf professionally today. She also dedicates much of her time to motivational speaking, mentorship courses, and mother-daughter retreats to help empower women and girls to overcome their own challenges.[6]

Confidence: Confidence gives you the belief that you can achieve all the above. You need self-confidence to truly believe that you can control your emotions in difficult situations and can commit and follow through on the goals you set, and the knowledge that you are up for any challenge. Confidence is not arrogance. It is not an out-of-control ego and an unwillingness to accept feedback or constructive criticism. Rather, confidence allows you to look objectively at your areas of strength and weakness, with the conviction that you can make the necessary improvements to continue to move toward achieving your goals.

Born to a poor, unwed teenage mother in rural Mississippi in the 1950s, Oprah Winfrey was raised on her grandmother's farm as a young child before being sent to live with her mother in Milwaukee in a small inner-city apartment. While her mother worked long hours as a maid, Oprah was repeatedly sexually abused by men who were known to her mother. She later moved to Nashville as an adolescent to live with her father after years of instability and uncertainty.

Despite her difficult childhood, Oprah knew she was destined for more. She became the first African American news anchor in Nashville at the age of 19. She then followed that up with a move to Chicago to host a morning talk show that would eventually become the Oprah Winfrey Show. Her show would run for 25 seasons, and its success helped her to become the world's first Black, female billionaire and the world's only Black billionaire for three years running, from 2003. Oprah Winfrey has used her success to launch several business and philanthropic endeavors, dedicating much of her influence to shining a light on the topic of sexual abuse.[7]

Despite the challenges Oprah faced as a child, her inner confidence pushed her toward the success she enjoys today, and she serves as an inspiration for others.

Implementing the four Cs of mental toughness and seeing the impact they can have on your life is just the tip of the iceberg of what mental toughness can help you achieve. They unlock the secret formula to being more effective and successful in all areas of life. Who doesn't want that?

Many people today are struggling to juggle work, personal life, and leisure activities. No matter how hard they try, they can't quite seem to make it all work. More and more people spend their adult lives feeling burnt out and defeated by life. They are stuck in mediocre or unfulfilling jobs and can't seem to find the time to create the fulfilling personal lives they would like to have. They keep doing the same things and getting the same disappointing results.

Sound familiar? Ready to make a change? Developing mental toughness is not something that happens overnight, nor is it something you achieve once and never think about again. It is a mindset, a way of perceiving and reacting to the world around you that will replace any self-defeating or negative strategies you may currently be using as a way to get through the day.

Sounds like a lot of work. Is it really worth it?

Absolutely!

<u>Benefits of Developing Mental Toughness</u>

Research has identified multiple benefits of a mental toughness mentality. Mentally tough individuals are identified with being more likely to be sociable, calm, and relaxed, with lower levels of stress and anxiety. It is also associated with lower levels of depression and higher levels of life satisfaction.[8]

Sounds counterintuitive, considering that mentally tough people are also known for being competitive, persistent, and resilient. They are associated with overcoming some of the biggest difficulties life can throw at them. Let's look more closely at why this is.

In a professional setting, mental toughness and its associated traits are associated with enhanced work performance, better decision-making capabilities, and greater confidence. The profile of mentally tough employees tends to be ambitious but not aggressive, with enhanced intrapersonal skills and higher productivity, leading to greater organizational success.[9]

In addition, mental toughness is thought to influence how people respond to stress, pressure, opportunities, and challenges. It corresponds to an enhanced ability to cope with failure, Mentally tough employees are more likely to contribute to a positive organizational culture, and to report increased job satisfaction.[10]

Mental toughness isn't just suited to professional environments. Benefits are seen in all aspects of life. Mentally tough people are likely to spend time working on their self-awareness, meaning they are clear on what's important to them. So often people are superstars at work, only to struggle to hold onto personal relationships, whether with romantic partners, other family members, or friends. Finding the right balance starts with having clear priorities in life.

Mental Toughness vs. Resilience

Isn't mental toughness just being resilient? Actually, no. It is often mistaken for resilience, but mental toughness embodies so much more. When we face adversity or challenges in life, there are three stages we must pass through.

1. Stage one is the pre-adversity stage, where we either see something coming on the horizon or are blissfully oblivious to the storm that's coming.

2. Stage two is the adverse event, the challenge we must face, like being in the thick of a massive storm.

3. Finally, stage three is the post-adversity stage where we deal with the fallout, the cleanup once the tornado has passed.

Mental toughness begins in stage one. It is living your life in a way that prepares you for life's challenges before they hit. Stage two is where grit comes in. Grit is the perseverance that helps you weather the storm and not crumble under the weight of it. Resilience is stage three. It is what helps you reduce the long-term burden of that event and bounce back to be able to keep moving forward.

Individuals who practice resilience without the other components of mental toughness can sometimes do more harm than good. It may lead to a false idea that admitting to needing help is a sign of weakness and that returning to normal as quickly as possible is the most important thing to do.

Mentally tough individuals are constantly aware of their emotions and use a variety of strategies to keep them under control. Mentally tough people don't just survive under pressure, they thrive! Mental toughness uses resilience as just one of many tools to help move beyond the mere ability to survive adversity. What happens after you bounce back? You return to stage one! Mentally tough individuals often weather life's storms more successfully than those who aren't, and have an easier time recovering from them.

They then employ a variety of other traits to move to a place where they see adversity as an opportunity to learn, grow, and excel under pressure. They are able to see beyond the short-term difficulty to the long-term benefit of successfully navigating new challenges. As a result, they are seen as valuable contributors in the workplace and in their personal relationships rather than as victims or martyrs.

Action Steps

To get the most out of this book, each chapter will have a series of action steps for you to take before moving to the next chapter. Cultivating mental toughness means not just learning about what it takes but taking action to develop it and practicing the skills over time.

1. Tackle something head-on. Is there an activity or task that you have been avoiding out of discomfort or fear? Choose something small enough to tackle this week, schedule it on your calendar, and get it done! Confronting challenges helps build confidence and improves our resilience in the face of discomfort.

2. Learn to Fail. Let's face it, nobody likes to fail. But mentally tough people can look at failure dispassionately and learn from it. They apply those lessons to their next challenge. This week, choose a low-stakes activity in which you know you are likely to fail, perhaps in your free time. Have you always wanted to learn to play guitar? Or to surf? Speak a new language? Give yourself permission to try something and fail at it the first time, and then see what you can learn from it.

Just like LeBron James, developing mental toughness can help you unlock your full potential, whether it's on the court like him, in your career, or in your personal life. Beyond resilience, it embodies traits of positive psychology that allow you to view life's challenges as opportunities to grow and thrive. And it all starts with the secret ingredient explained in Chapter 2, Mindset.

Chapter Summary

- Mental toughness is mastering the four Cs:
  Control, Commitment, Challenge, and
  Confidence.

- The practice of mental toughness is not limited to the world of sports.
- Mental toughness is beneficial for improving all areas of life, including at work, at home, and during leisure activities.
- It is the ability to manage and overcome difficulties in life while maintaining a positive outlook.
- Mental toughness goes beyond resilience, to not just overcome adversity, but to thrive in the face of it.

2

THE MIND'S INFLUENCE

THE STRATEGIES FOR TURNING YOUR FIXED MINDSET INTO A GROWTH MINDSET

What if I told you that most of what you have been taught to believe about talent, intelligence, skill, and ability is wrong?

How often have you looked at someone else's success in a specific area, and chalked it up to talent? Natural ability? Innate intelligence? *He's a talented athlete; he was born to be a superstar! She's a natural leader! He was born with the voice of an angel!*

How often have you looked at your own shortcomings and done the same? *I wish I had the talent to be an artist! I'm terrible at math. I may as well not even try. Public speaking is terrifying. I'll never be good at it.*

Do you believe that things like intelligence or ability are set in stone? It can seem that some people are just naturally endowed with certain personality traits or talents that virtually guarantee them success in that area, and that some are not. Are you afraid of trying new things because you are worried that you won't be any good at them?

If so, you may have a fixed mindset. And that is hindering your ability to develop mental toughness.

Maybe you think that some of those statements are true, but not all. You may have a hybrid mindset, where some areas are growth-oriented, and others are stuck in a fixed mentality.

The good news is that a fixed mindset doesn't have to remain, well, fixed. A growth mindset can be cultivated, and this book will show you how.

The Power of Mindset: Fixed vs Growth

Mindset is really the building block upon which all other aspects of one's life are constructed. A mindset, at its core, is just a powerful belief system. How you see yourself shapes how you see the world. If you believe that you can continue to learn, develop, and grow throughout your life, the way you see life's challenges begins to shift. Rather than lamenting shortcomings or obstacles to success, a person who believes in the power of possibility will view those obstacles as opportunities and begin making plans to overcome them. That's the power of a growth mindset.

<u>Fixed Mindset</u>

The defining characteristic of a fixed mindset is the belief that much of who we are, including our talents, skills, and abilities, is out of our control and essentially set in stone. Much importance is placed on things like natural talent or IQ tests that measure intelligence as though it were something unchangeable. The fixed mindset puts people into categories that are seen as largely permanent.

Rather than believing that a skill can be learned or improved over time and with much dedication, fixed mindset individuals believe that you either have ability or you don't.

As a result, many people with fixed mindsets get caught up in their identity being tied to skills or talents that may or may not change over time. If you were labeled the smart kid at school or the musical prodigy as a child, that identity can not only be a source of pride but can become a source of insecurity over time.

What happens when the smart kid fails a test? Or when the musical prodigy is no longer considered a prodigy as they age, and other musicians catch up to their level of skill?

Fixed-mindset individuals constantly feel the need to prove themselves and don't tend to cope well with hardship, failure, or rejection. They are afraid of making mistakes or showing weakness. In personal relationships, they often search for someone who will make them feel special and engage their need for validation.[1]

<u>Growth Mindset</u>

Perhaps the defining characteristic of a growth mindset is the belief that a person's true potential is unknown, and that where you are right now is nothing but a starting point for continued self-improvement. Not to be mistaken for toxic positivity or for a refusal to see things for what they are, a growth mindset is about facing reality, not pretending that things are different than they are.

Individuals with a growth mindset focus on self-improvement, take responsibility for their actions, and look for solutions to problems rather than blame others for their own shortcomings. This leads to several benefits that those with fixed mindsets don't enjoy.

Studies have shown that those with growth mindsets are better able to accurately assess their own abilities compared with those with a fixed mindset. They understand that those abilities are not set in stone and can be developed over time, so someone with a growth mindset doesn't feel the need to embellish the truth.[2]

A growth mindset is more conducive to the development of a greater tolerance for frustration and more resilience in the face of setbacks. People with a growth mindset believe more strongly in the possibility of human potential.

In relationships, they search for partners that will encourage them to keep growing and learning. They look for friends who stretch their horizons. Growth-mindset individuals aren't interested in always being the smartest person in the room. They enjoy the challenge of learning from others in the room and surround themselves with interesting people.

In the workplace, a growth mindset is found to be positively correlated to a greater ability to develop adaptive skills to cope with career-related challenges. It is also associated with improved employee performance, greater leadership abilities, and higher levels of work engagement and motivation.[3] Those with a growth mindset show more grit, passion, and perseverance to not abandon tasks in the face of adversity.

A longitudinal study of over 10,000 cadets at the U.S. Military Academy at West Point studied the impact of cognitive ability (higher intelligence), physical ability, and grit on both the short-term likelihood of completing the six-week initial initiation training and continuing to graduate from the four-year program.

They found that cadets who scored higher on the cognitive attribute scale were more likely to get higher academic grades in the program over the long term. However, neither higher-scoring cognitive nor physical abilities were the best predictors of both short- or long-term success in the program.

It was grit. Angela Duckworth defines grit as a combination of passion and perseverance for a singularly important goal, and believes that it is the hallmark of high achievers in every domain.[4]

Cadets who scored higher in grit than the average were more likely to complete both the initial six-week training program and to go on to successfully graduate from the four-year program. Intelligence and physical talent helped cadets move toward some of the goals, but the cadets with grit were able to believe in their abilities and keep going when things got tough.[5]

The following table provides a brief comparison of how a growth-mindset individual and a fixed-mindset individual may perceive certain attributes.

Attribute	Growth	Fixed
Intelligence	Intelligence is malleable and can be increased with effort and studying. *"With a study plan and the right support, I can improve my understanding of any subject."*	Intelligence is fixed. People are smart in some areas, not in others. *"I'm not good at languages. I could never learn French."*
Athletic Ability	Some people may be naturally athletic, but anyone can improve their ability with the right training. *"I want to run a marathon next year, so I'll set goals and track my progress."*	Athletes are born with a talent for the sport. Without that natural talent, nobody can be that good. *"I wasn't born with athletic ability. I could never run a marathon."*
Musical Talent	Some people have an ear for music, but anyone can practice an instrument enough to become proficient. *"Some theories say it takes 10,000 hours of practice to master a new skill. I'll start with two hours of piano practice a week and see where it takes me."*	Musical talent is inherited or passed down. Prodigies are born, not made. *"I'm tone deaf and can't sing on pitch if I try. There's no use trying to pick up an instrument as an adult."*
Receiving Feedback	Feedback is welcomed and seen as an opportunity for improvement. *"My boss had a lot of excellent feedback to help me improve my presentation skills. I'm looking forward to putting them into practice."*	Fight or flight response. Feedback is something to dread and to be avoided at all costs. *"My boss is out to get me and nitpicked every little thing on my year-end evaluation. I can't wait until he isn't my manager anymore."*
Success of Others	Acknowledges and encourages the success of others. Finds inspiration in their achievements. *"He worked hard for that promotion. This time next year I want to be promoted too."*	Feels threatened by the success of others and brushes it off or finds a reason why they were undeserving of their success. *"He didn't deserve his promotion. Everybody knows the boss plays favorites."*
Accepting Failure	Failure is something to learn from. Success often follows multiple failures, so don't give up. *"I am disappointed that I didn't get the result I wanted, but I know that I can learn from this result and do better next time."*	Failure is a sign of weakness. It's easier to give up than to try and fail again. *"I failed the test because I'm no good at math. This class is stupid."*

Strategies for Developing a Growth Mindset and Overcoming Obstacles

Here are three strategies you can implement today to start you on the path to developing a growth mindset.

Banish negative self-talk

Developing a growth mindset means leaving your limiting beliefs behind. Practicing self-reflection and reframing negative self-talk are the first steps in identifying your limiting beliefs, reframing them to become actionable items.

Many of us engage in negative self-talk so much that we don't even catch ourselves when we do it. Once we start paying attention, it's easy to become discouraged when we realize just how frequently it occurs.

One technique for reframing negative self-talk begins with acknowledging the thought without judgment. Next, actively reject it as false, replacing it with one that is kinder and more growth-oriented.

This practice takes time and requires self-awareness and self-compassion. Try imagining a small child being told some of the same negative things you tell yourself. What would you tell that child instead? You deserve to treat yourself with the same kindness.

Manage stress

Stress is an inevitable part of life, so trying to eliminate stress is unrealistic and ultimately unhelpful. A certain amount of stress can have a positive impact and help motivate individuals to accomplish tasks and goals.

Unmanageable, chronic stress levels do the opposite and are a hallmark of the fixed mindset that fears anything other than praise and perfection. While living off the adrenaline rush of meeting deadlines at the last minute or having a schedule that doesn't allow for any downtime might be sustainable for a short period, eventually, it catches up.

The effects of long-term chronic stress are detrimental to one's physical and mental health and can show up as chronic illness, depression, anxiety, or other mental health concerns.

Managing stress and prioritizing self-care may seem counterproductive, but the long-term benefits of an employee, partner, or friend who is not buckling under the stress in their life are significant. A morning or nighttime guided meditation, a daily walk or short workout, getting outside for 15 minutes a day, journaling, or even making time daily for 10 minutes of quiet time can go a long way. When you are less stressed, you are more positive and ready to face challenges with a growth mindset.

<u>Learn to love feedback</u>

This strategy is more difficult to implement than the last two and therefore requires more explanation. One of the most common and relevant stories about handling criticism or feedback of any kind features a bucket, water, sand, and, if you're lucky, gold.

Whenever we receive criticism or feedback that isn't completely positive, it feels like getting hit in the face with a bucket full of water with a few inches of sand at the bottom. The water is shockingly cold, and often catches us by surprise. It is followed by the gritty, wet sand that scratches our face and stings our eyes. We are often shocked and uncomfortable and find it hard to catch our breath.

The first response is often either fight or flight. Sometimes we lash out at the person holding the bucket, defending ourselves against feedback we deem to be harsh or unfair. Other times we simply try to get it all off, wringing the water out of our clothes and brushing the sand away frantically so we can make a quick exit and forget it ever happened.

Fixed-mindset individuals almost always choose one of the two options above. Feedback or criticism is typically avoided at all costs, as anything other than being seen as perfect is considered a threat. Taking the fight option can lead to defending our position at all costs, even when we suspect we may not be completely justified in doing so. The fight response can see us lash out and try to tear down the other person, bringing up their own faults to take the attention off our own. This can be particularly devastating in personal relationships.

When a person with a fixed mindset chooses flight instead, they try to separate themselves from the criticism or feedback altogether. They may come up with reasons why the feedback is wrong or spend time justifying their own stance to themselves to feel better. The person giving the feedback can feel dismissed or ignored, and the relationship can be damaged. In a work environment, this can lead to strained working relationships and stunted progress. In the end, the person giving the feedback does not see any positive change, and the person refusing to take the feedback misses the opportunity to learn and grow.

What happens next?

Some continue as though no feedback was given at all. For others, they become fixated on the water and sand and take it all to heart. Rather than using feedback constructively, they view it as confirmation of their deepest fear that they are a failure. Their confidence is damaged, and they may begin to feel insecure in other areas of life as well.

There is a third option.

Remember our bucket? As the story goes, in most buckets of criticism or feedback, some gold is mixed in somewhere with the sand. The gold may come in the form of large nuggets or be hidden away as tiny flakes, but if one looks closely enough, there's usually some gold somewhere.

The gold is the truth, the feedback that you want to hold onto. Constructive criticism sometimes hurts the most, but it can have the biggest positive impact if you can face it. People with a growth mindset are the ones who, once the water has been toweled off and the sand has been wiped from the eyes, look for the gold.[6]

Individuals with a growth mindset, who are mentally tough, look at feedback and constructive criticism as an opportunity for improvement. Rather than fearing it, defending against it, or running from it, they welcome the opportunity to take their performance to the next level. This is as true for workplace feedback as it is for feedback in a personal relationship or for improvement while learning a new skill during leisure activities. When viewed as an opportunity, a lack of feedback is more disappointing than tough feedback. Those with a growth mindset don't dwell on the negative and allow criticism to feed into their insecurities.

Choosing the third option isn't the safe or easy choice. Self-protection in the form of fight or flight is the easier choice, and the ones most taken by fixed-mindset individuals. They are also the least effective, most self-sabotaging choices. It takes mental toughness and a strong belief in the potential for improvement that a growth mindset offers to choose option three. Which option do you currently choose? Is it helping or hindering your personal growth?

Action Steps

1. Start practicing self-reflection: Doing the work to improve your mindset can be a bit daunting. Consider a method of keeping track of your successes and failures, and how you feel along the way is a great way to practice self-compassion, reframe negative thoughts, and track your progress. Choose a method that works with your personality and will be easy to keep up. A journal, note on your phone, quick voice note, or sketch are all great ways to start the self-reflection habit.

2. Seek out feedback: Accepting feedback and seeing it as an opportunity for real improvement is not always easy. If this is particularly difficult for you, start small with someone you trust. Over the next month, ask for feedback on one small, less personal topic from someone close to you daily. Gradually widen both the circle of people you seek feedback from and the range of topics you seek the feedback on. Use your self-reflection practice to track how you respond to feedback over time.

3. Shake it off: Is there a label you were given as a child that you struggle to shake off? How do your beliefs around this label continue to hinder you? What steps could you take to begin changing your beliefs around it?

Your mindset is a powerful belief system about your locus of control. Fixed-mindset individuals are more likely to believe that things happen to them, while those with a growth mindset believe that they are the ones who make things happen. In Chapter 3, we'll take this idea to the next level and get real about where you stand right now, where you want to be, and how you're going to get there.

Chapter Summary

- A growth mindset is essential for developing mental toughness.
- A growth mindset is the belief that your abilities and skills can be developed and improved over time and with practice and effort.
- A fixed mindset is the belief that your essential abilities and skills, such as intelligence, are fixed and can only be changed slightly, if at all.
- It is possible to have a hybrid mindset, where you believe that certain qualities are fixed, and others can be changed.
- Obstacles such as a fear of making mistakes, looking weak, or failing, can stop people from starting on the path to a growth mindset.
- Engaging strategies such as reframing negative self-talk, managing stress, and learning to embrace feedback can help overcome obstacles and cultivate a growth mindset.

3

THE POWER OF SELF-REFLECTION
DISCOVERING STRATEGIES TO TURN YOUR
THOUGHTS AND BEHAVIOR INTO MENTAL
TOUGHNESS ADVANTAGES

"I don't think you're quite ready for the promotion just yet. I know you were hoping for it, but there are some key objectives you are still struggling to meet. I had hoped you would have been able to reach them by now. I'll tell you what, rather than meeting again in a year, let's revisit this in six months and see where you stand."

Mihaela's manager said a few more things that she couldn't focus on before wrapping up the employee review meeting because her mind was reeling from the bad news. This was the second time she was denied a promotion, with "failure to meet key objectives" as one of the reasons for denying her what she felt she deserved.

She struggled to finish the meeting and sign her review before heading to the bathroom to calm down and get herself together for the rest of the workday.

"What am I doing wrong?" she asked herself. Her emotions ran rampant. Shock, surprise, sadness, embarrassment, anger, defiance – she struggled to make sense of it all. As she took a few deep breaths, what settled was shame.

She was ashamed that her boss didn't think her performance was up to par. She was ashamed of having to stay in the same position for at least another six months after having been denied a promotion twice in a row. And she was ashamed that her coworkers would know what had happened.

"What am I going to do now?" she thought.

What should she do now? How can Mihaela turn things around and be ready for that promotion at the next employee review in six months?

Patterns of Thought and Behavior

While she may not feel like it at the moment, Mihaela is in charge of what happens next. She can continue on the current path that she's on, putting in the same effort and getting the same disappointing results, or she can choose differently. Rather than rush to action however, she first needs to spend time understanding herself.

Making lifestyle or workplace changes without having a true understanding of your strengths, weaknesses, cognitive biases, thought patterns, and goals is like throwing wet spaghetti at the wall to see what sticks. It's a colossal waste of time and can do more harm than good. Rather than racing to climb the first ladder you see, you want to make sure that it is leaning against the right wall.

Let's start with cognitive bias because until we are seeing things clearly, we can't move forward in a meaningful way.

<u>Cognitive Bias</u>

Cognitive bias is when we take information and interpret it based on our own personal experiences or beliefs rather than based on a reasoned, objective assessment of the facts. Those experiences or beliefs are often based on selective memory, social pressure, or emotional associations. They can even be based on a process of mental shortcuts called heuristics that use previous knowledge to process and respond to new information quickly, based on prior knowledge. The problem with cognitive bias is that the assessments we make are not only not always accurate, but they can be steeped in incorrect information or stereotypes of which we are not consciously aware.[1]

While cognitive bias can sometimes be helpful, such as when we need to make snap decisions in an emergency situation, most of the time it works against us. We must identify and work to eliminate these biases in order to continue to grow and develop on the road to mental toughness. Holding onto our cognitive biases once we are aware of them is closing ourselves off to growth. When we break free of our rigid beliefs, we open up a world of knowledge and possibility that we were previously unable to see.

While more than 150 types of cognitive bias have been formally identified, even confronting a few of the most common ones can make a difference. Let's look at three specific cognitive biases that can have a strong impact on areas such as decision-making and problem-solving.

Self-Serving Bias

Self-Serving Bias is one of the most common, and most damaging to personal growth. Self-Serving Bias is true to its name. You interpret situations in the way that best serves you and your ego. When something good happens, you take credit for making it happen, whether or not you had anything to do with it.

On the flip side, when something awful or unwanted happens, you find a way to blame external forces for the occurrence, avoiding taking any personal responsibility. Much like the fight or flight response to feedback we discussed in the last chapter, self-serving cognitive bias allows us to put our heads in the sand and ignore that which is unpleasant.

Optimism Bias

The next common type of cognitive bias is optimism bias. Optimism bias can be a tricky one. It refers to the tendency to believe that you have less of a chance of failing or having terrible things happen to you than others. As a result, you may take chances that are based on little more than a good feeling, or without doing due diligence because of the belief that nothing truly bad will happen. This can be particularly dangerous when used in financial or business decisions, where a lack of a thorough risk assessment can spell disaster.

The difficulty for many with this particular cognitive bias is the way that having a positive outlook is typically seen as a strength. In much of the literature on mental toughness, working on changing from a negative to a positive mindset is seen as one of the key components to developing mental toughness. Seeing challenges as opportunities, and having the perseverance to push through them are cornerstones of the mentality. At first glance, it seems only fitting that having some degree of optimism bias would be required.

However, there is a big difference between a positive mindset and optimism bias. Having a positive mindset is a general state of mind in which one sees the world through the lens of possibility. But possibility does not mean delusion, nor does it mean ignoring facts. A person with a positive mindset can examine a situation objectively, and then put in motion a plan of action that aims to make the best of the situation.

A person with optimism bias ignores any facts that contradict what they want to hear, or simply doesn't believe those facts or risk factors apply to them. They are somehow more special than others, and the rules do not apply. They focus only on what they want to see, and simply dismiss what they don't as unimportant or unlikely to happen.

Confirmation Bias

The third common type of bias that hinders the development of mental toughness is confirmation bias. Similar to optimism bias, confirmation bias looks only at the positive. However, unlike optimism bias, which is rooted in the belief that the person is somehow more special than others and thereby unlikely to have bad things happen, confirmation bias is rooted in what the person chooses to focus on.

A person using confirmation bias will, whether consciously or unconsciously, seek out information that confirms their already formed beliefs or ideas. They may choose to only read or watch news media that confirm their stance on a variety of topics, surround themselves only with people who share similar beliefs about things that are important to them, or discount any information or opinions that differ from their own. In many ways, this bias relies almost on an invisible circle of protection that filters out any influences that don't completely fit in with our personal beliefs.[2]

In our personal lives, this could look like only socializing with people from our own ethnic, religious, or political groups. Over time, this can lead to close-minded points of view and a heightened sense of us and them. In the workplace, confirmation bias can lead to stagnation over innovation, and employees that have difficulty collaborating with others of different generations, backgrounds, or experiences.

Everyone exhibits cognitive bias from time to time. Our brains are confronted with an incredible amount of information and stimuli on a daily basis, and we often rely on our memories, experiences, and information to help us make many of the thousands of small decisions we make each day. If we have been treated poorly at the same café twice in the past, we may decide that it is an unwelcoming place and choose to never go in again. For decisions as small and inconsequential as this, relying on cognitive bias probably won't do us much harm.

It's when we allow it to get in the way of important issues that it becomes harmful to ourselves, and potentially to others. Taking the credit for things that were not our doing, or passing the blame for failures onto something or someone else instead of taking responsibility for our own shortcomings or errors is far more serious.

Ignoring red flags or other warning signs because we believe that we could never end up suffering to the same extent as others is irresponsible and can have long-term consequences. Choosing to only focus on information that confirms what we want to be true rather than what is true is both narrow-minded and divisive in all areas of life.[3]

Negative Thought Patterns

Identifying and changing negative thought patterns is one of the most powerful ways to positively impact several areas of your life simultaneously. What you think, and the tone of those thoughts, can vary throughout the course of the day and in response to different people, situations, and environments. While some people with severe depression or anxiety, or living in extremely stressful life circumstances may have predominantly negative thought patterns, for many people these patterns tend to be interspersed with more neutral or positive ones.

It has been argued that a symbiotic relationship exists between thought patterns, physical environment or life situation, mood, physical reactions, and outward behaviors. By symbiotic, I mean that the influence does not just flow in one direction. Our thoughts have an impact on the four areas mentioned above, but those four factors also impact our thoughts.[4]

Let's go back to Mihaela and her passed-over promotion. How has she handled the disappointment in the weeks following her employee review?

Environment/Life Situation: Mihaela has been passed over for a promotion at her job twice in a row. She really wants to move up the corporate ladder, but now has serious doubts about her ability to do so following her latest missed promotion. She spends her days thinking about how she's never going to get promoted and will be stuck in her current job until she retires. As a result, she stops signing up for optional training opportunities, avoids socializing with her colleagues out of embarrassment, and puts less effort into her work since she no longer sees the point. As a result, she has less mental space for actually doing her work and doing it well. This impedes her future potential for promotion.

Mood: Mihaela's colleagues have noticed that she always seems to be in a bad mood these days. The more Mihaela thinks about her work situation, the more she feels embarrassed, discouraged, and hopeless about her situation. She has withdrawn from all but the essential tasks of her job.

Physical Reaction: Whenever Mihaela thinks about the meeting where she was informed that she was not chosen for the most recent promotion, her chest constricts, her body tenses, and she has an overwhelming desire to leave the office. She avoids eye contact with her manager and colleagues whenever possible.

Behavior: Mihaela hasn't been herself since being passed over for promotion. She rehashes the employee evaluation meeting on her way to work each day, and often at night before going to bed. She finds it hard to fall asleep and wakes up tired most mornings. She used to bring coffee in for the office on Fridays, but she has not done that since that meeting. She eats lunch alone at her desk and turns down opportunities to join the team on their monthly after-work social activity. She has distanced herself both emotionally and physically from her entire work team.

Changing Negative Thought Patterns

It is obvious that for Mihaela to start feeling better, she needs to change her negative thought patterns.

Except that's just the beginning. Just as environment, mood, physical reactions, and behavior are influenced by thoughts, so too are thoughts influenced by those factors. In order to effect real change, it often takes more than just replacing unhappy or negative thoughts with positive ones.[5]

Let me explain.

Mihaela probably notices her negative thought patterns. She thinks about her disappointment and shame around her job on the way to work, when she sees her manager and colleagues, when she turns down invitations for lunch or socializing, and before she goes to sleep at night. In Mihaela's case, the negative thoughts are not subconscious, but front and center in her world.

Changing her negative thoughts to positive ones will help in some ways. Perhaps by journaling, meditating, or replacing negative thoughts about her situation with positive ones, she will be able to improve her mood somewhat, and to avoid the negative physical reactions she is currently experiencing upon entering the work environment. Likewise, she can choose to return to her old behaviors of bringing coffee into the office for her colleagues on Fridays and attending the monthly social gatherings.

However, all the positive thoughts in the world won't be enough to significantly change her circumstances and do what she needs to do to move forward in her career. For that, she needs to use the power of positive thinking to actually effect change in her situation.

First step? Mihaela can first identify and address any cognitive biases she may be employing that are not working in her favor.

Did she believe that she truly could not be passed over for promotion twice in a row (optimism bias)? Is she blaming someone or something else for her failure to secure the promotion, such as her manager not liking her (self-serving bias)? Was she only looking at the signs supporting her belief that she would be promoted and not the ones contradicting that view (confirmation bias)?

Once she becomes aware of the biased lens through which she has possibly been viewing her career, she can see more clearly exactly where her beliefs strayed from the reality of the situation.

What comes next?

A personal SWOT analysis.

Creating a Personal SWOT Analysis

SWOT is an acronym for Strengths, Weaknesses, Opportunities, and Threats. SWOT analysis is a tool originally designed to help businesses optimize performance and minimize risk, while managing competition and making better business decisions. It evaluates both the internal factors of strengths and weaknesses and the external forces of opportunities and threats to create a comprehensive picture of where a business stands. SWOT analysis is a simple but effective tool that is then used to create a plan of action for moving forward. Though originally developed for business, it is also applicable to various other fields, including the area of personal growth.[6]

It is important to note that a SWOT analysis is typically completed to assess a specific area of concern, rather than as a general diagnostic tool. What does that mean? Well, when creating a personal SWOT analysis, it may make more sense to complete one for your job and another for a specific area of concern in your personal life, as the strengths, weaknesses, opportunities, and threats may look very different.

Let's take a look at each area a bit more in-depth.

<u>Strengths</u>: These are the areas in which you shine! Mental toughness, a growth mindset, and self-awareness are strengths that are useful in all situations. Strengths can be general traits applicable across many areas of life, or more specific skill-related items. For example, in a work context, skills specific to your job, such as technology skills, may be relevant. On the other hand, when conducting a SWOT analysis of your marriage, being an expert in spreadsheets is probably not valued in quite the same way!

<u>Weaknesses</u>: To be effective, it's important to be completely honest when filling out this section. It can be hard to see our weaknesses laid bare, but when we look at

them as challenges to overcome and areas for growth, they become less intimidating. We really need to clear away the cognitive biases on this one and be super self-aware in order to stretch ourselves to the fullest.

It's important to note that self-awareness isn't about wallowing over faults, but about being realistic about where we need to put our efforts in order to achieve our goals. Are you prone to procrastination or distraction? Or is there a specific work skill you know you should learn but have never made the time? Write them down!

Strengths and weaknesses are the internal factors in the SWOT analysis. These are the aspects that you bring to the table and have complete control over.

Now let's look at the external factors.

<u>Opportunities</u>: Opportunities are those chances that we must act on in order to reap the benefits. Returning to Mihaela, she saw the opportunity for promotion. However, maybe there were other work opportunities she missed out on because she was solely focused on that particular promotion. Don't be afraid to look outside your comfort zone and identify things that may be a little intimidating. The purpose of a SWOT analysis is to encourage growth.

<u>Threats</u>: Identifying threats is understanding which battles must be fought, and where you are most at risk. Threats are typically seen as factors outside your immediate environment that may hold you back in the future, such as your job eventually being replaced by

technology. However, your immediate environment and the people in it can also be threats right now. Sometimes threats can be linked to your areas of weakness. The key is to try and identify threats ahead of time, so that you can make a plan to neutralize them at worst, or turn them into opportunities at best.

Returning to the case of Mihaela, once she faces her cognitive biases, she can then create a work-specific SWOT analysis, analyzing her strengths, weaknesses, opportunities, and threats as they relate to her career. Mihaela can then apply the results of her SWOT analysis to change her circumstances.

She may create a plan to work on her weaknesses in order to be better qualified for the promotion within the revised six-month period. She may realize that the promotion she wanted isn't actually best suited to her strengths and set her sights on a different role. Or she may realize that her current place of employment has more threats than opportunities and choose to orient her plan to moving to another company or even another industry in the near future.

Whichever path Mihaela chooses, she will need to develop both her self-confidence and resilience to set and achieve goals, rather than have them remain as vague dreams. She will then need to employ the 4 Cs of mental toughness, Control, Commitment, Challenge, and Confidence, to work diligently towards those goals.

Action Steps

1. Change your thought patterns. Negative thought patterns affect everyone from time to time, but they can get in the way of the progress we have been working so hard to achieve. Try the following three-step practice to reframe negative thought patterns into positive ones: 1- acknowledge the thought and recognize it for what it is, usually your mind's attempt to protect you from perceived harm; 2- release the thought without judgment; 3- replace the thought with a positive, yet realistic one.

2. Combat cognitive bias. Seek out information that challenges your beliefs. For the next month, incorporate a news source into your daily rotation with a point of view that is opposite to what you usually consume. Keep a log of how the news coverage makes you feel, which points you reject immediately, and whether you are able to better understand where they are coming from over time. The purpose is not to change your general beliefs, but to begin looking at things from a different perspective.

3. Know where you stand. Complete a personal SWOT analysis. Make it specific to one area of life, such as work, to get the most accurate results. Repeat for other areas of life you feel would benefit from this tool.

What to do with all this clarity you now have? Prepare yourself for the hard work of making change happen! In Chapter 4, we'll learn exactly how to cultivate and project the image we want the world to see. We will also help you build the resilience needed to make that image a reality so that you will be ready to define your goals and make them happen.

Chapter Summary

- Self-awareness helps you to better understand your strengths and weaknesses and to use that information to develop mental toughness and cope with challenges.
- Cognitive bias can negatively affect decision-making and problem-solving skills and hinder personal growth if unaddressed.
- Developing a personal SWOT analysis (Strengths, Weaknesses, Opportunities, and Threats) can inform strategies for building a structured approach to personal improvement and growth.
- For maximum benefits, consider conducting a SWOT analysis in different areas of life, one for work, another for personal life

4

SELF-CONFIDENCE IS THE KEY

DISCOVER HOW CONFIDENCE CAN GIVE AN EXTRA ADVANTAGE WHEN DEVELOPING MENTAL TOUGHNESS

Last chapter, we talked about Mihaela and her work woes. Rather than wallow in despair, Mihaela has a host of opportunities available to her to take her success into her own hands. She could remove her cognitive biases, perform a personal SWOT analysis of her current situation, and break out of her negative mindset. The big question is, *Will Mihaela have the confidence to start and the resilience to see it through?*

A key element of mental toughness is self-confidence which, at its core, is the belief and self-trust individuals have in their ability to face adversity. Part of that self-trust is built through the development of resilience, both individually and in concert with others. Everyone has the potential to achieve great things. Not everyone has the confidence to even try, and fewer still have the mental toughness to see their efforts through to the end.

But that doesn't have to be you!

This chapter will teach you the secret to exuding confidence even under the most difficult circumstances.

How to Be the Most Confident Person in the Room

Have you ever noticed how some people seem to command a room without saying a word? They have an aura about them that is hard to define. They carry themselves differently and seem unphased by even the most intimidating circumstances. Confidence carries its own weight.

The bad news? It doesn't come naturally to everyone.

The good news? Absolutely anyone can develop it.

Confident people aren't fundamentally different from everyone else. They have just developed belief in themselves, and you can too. In this chapter, we'll discuss the difference between self-confidence and self-esteem, and why both are needed to be mentally tough. We'll learn tried and true ways to work on developing both. We'll examine why negative self-talk is so common, and how to turn it around. Finally, we'll connect all of the above to resilience and find out why building resilience isn't a solitary sport.

What is self-confidence?

At its essence, self-confidence refers to your trust in your own skills, abilities, and judgments. A self-confident person trusts in their ability to rise to challenges, believing that they have the character and skill to be successful.

They also believe that they genuinely have a certain measure of control over certain aspects of life.[1] Self-confidence involves a high degree of self-awareness, including intimate knowledge of your personal set of resources and skills, and an awareness of your impact on others.[2]

Self-confident individuals have been found to score higher on happiness scales, have better job satisfaction in middle age, higher energy and motivation levels, and lower levels of fear, anxiety, and stress than those who don't. They even tend to have higher survival rates following major surgery![3] It is important to note that self-confidence must be accompanied by self-awareness, or it risks crossing the line into narcissism and fragility. Confidence must be based on an accurate assessment of our skills and abilities. This means learning to fail well and to learn from our failures in order to bounce back stronger.

What is self-esteem?

If self-confidence is the outward, visible manifestation of one's belief in their abilities, self-esteem can be considered the invisible manifestation.

Self-esteem is essentially how much you value and love yourself.[4] It can perhaps be described as your feeling of self-worth and self-respect. People with high self-esteem tend to be generally healthier, have greater mental well-being, and have more active social lives than those with low self-esteem.[5]

Self-esteem isn't tied to your skills and abilities, but rather your inherent worthiness as a human being. Life circumstances change, and our skills and abilities may change as well. If we have true self-esteem, these changes should not diminish how we feel about ourselves in relation to our self-love and acceptance.

Ideally, self-esteem and self-confidence should go hand-in-hand. These attributes seem so similar on the outside that they are often used interchangeably. However, this is not always the case. One can have a high level of self-esteem, but still be unconfident about their abilities in particular situations. Conversely, there are times when we are self-confident in certain circumstances as a result of training or experience, but generally suffer from low self-esteem.

To develop mental toughness, both must be cultivated and nurtured.

<u>Negative Self-Talk</u>

To open up the mental space to focus on developing self-confidence, we must first work on diminishing our internal negative self-talk. Earlier, we discussed negative mindsets, focusing on the thoughts we sometimes have that are directed externally, at people or situations.

Negative self-talk is similar but differs in an important way. Rather than being directed at external stimuli, it is instead turned inward. In that way, it is also more difficult to tame because we create and validate our beliefs about ourselves. As we already know, our thoughts and feelings influence each other. Negative self-talk negatively influences how we feel about ourselves. If we are dissatisfied with ourselves, it is difficult to disagree with our internal negative thoughts, and so the cycle continues.

Reframing Negative Self-Talk

Reframing negative self-talk is similar to changing negative thought patterns in general, only it can be more difficult because it can be hard to be objective about ourselves. It starts with becoming aware of our inner voice and questioning what it is telling us.

Where is the evidence that what I'm telling myself is true? Where's the evidence that maybe it's not? Sounds simple, but remember, negative self-talk isn't always based on facts. Watch out in particular for all-or-nothing statements like "I'm never going to get out of debt," or "Nobody will ever love me." Always, never, no one, everyone – they don't usually hold up to scrutiny.

Try reframing your statements to better reflect the feelings behind them. "I'm so far in debt I'm *afraid* that I'll never get out." "It's been so long since I've dated anyone that I'm *worried* I will never find another partner." Most of our negative self-talk is rooted in our insecurities. Once we are able to accurately identify the insecurity or emotion behind the statement, we can begin to change the narrative. Just acknowledging the emotion can be enough to take some of the sting out of the thought.

Notice that I didn't suggest you take a negative thought and randomly replace it with a positive one. That's because while sometimes our insecurities or worries are unfounded, sometimes they're based on real concerns. Pretending they aren't real and sugar-coating them in meaningless positive language can be unhelpful.

If you are deeply in debt, that can be scary and stressful. It's not negative to acknowledge those emotions, it's realistic. The transformative work comes from reframing the statement into a more realistic one that acknowledges the emotion behind the statement so that you can then begin dealing with the underlying issue.

What would happen if you didn't get out of debt? What steps could you take to begin reducing your current debt load? These are rational, relevant questions that address the concern without shifting into blaming or shaming territory.

Why is language so important anyway?

Excellent question. I mean, debt is debt, right? No amount of reframing a statement about being in debt is going to get me out of it. It makes no difference if I say it to myself nicely or not. Except that it does.

Language matters.

Language shapes human thought, cognitive abilities, perception, emotions, and decision-making abilities.[6] Language affects what and how we perceive things beyond the physical properties of what we can see.[7] A great example is the research around color perception, particularly distinguishing between blue and green and the shades in between.

In some languages, there is no distinction between the colors blue and green. In others, they are differentiated via a descriptor but not into separate colors. In English, blue and green are separate colors, and often shades are identified by adding another word, such as "light" blue, but not by renaming it entirely. Other languages have completely different color names for each shade.[8]

These labels serve to categorize colors and affect how we perceive them depending on the language we speak. People from languages that don't have several words for the various shades of blue and green have difficulty differentiating between them. The opposite is true for people whose language has several different words to identify them.

Interestingly, research has shown that by providing people with more color labels and more language to describe what they see, color perception can be altered.[9] Changing the number of color words available to them can improve people's ability to distinguish between colors. What they see can be affected by the language they have to describe it.

What does all this have to do with negative self-talk? Quite a lot, actually. That's because language plays a role in shaping cognition. Or, more simply put, the way we talk affects how we think.[10] It plays a role in all areas of human thought. If a difference in the words we use to describe colors changes how we actually see them, can you imagine how much of an impact the words we use to refer to ourselves would have on how we perceive our own self-worth?

The words we use when engaging in self-talk are perhaps the most important influence on how we perceive ourselves. We know from the previous chapter that language influences emotions, and emotions influence everything from decision-making abilities to physical reactions in our bodies. So while changing the way we talk to ourselves about our debt may not magically erase it from the books, it can make the difference between throwing our hands in the air and conceding defeat, or having the confidence to tackle the problem head-on.

Building Resilience

Resilience is the ability to successfully adapt to life's challenges, and to bounce back after challenging life experiences. The two main components involve an ability to face adversity and be able to positively adapt to challenging circumstances.[11] Resilience isn't something we miraculously find in difficult situations. It is a skill we cultivate during good times so that we can call on it when we need it.

What comes to mind when you think of resilience? What type of person comes to mind?

Did you picture a strong person in both mind and body, who fearlessly approached adversity with steely resolve? Or like the characters you see in movies who are a little mysterious, but always come through in a pinch?

The stereotype of the strong, silent type who shoulders an enormous amount of responsibility and hardship alone is not the most accurate depiction of what resilience looks like in the real world. In reality, resilience is not a solo sport. On the contrary, research shows that the most resilient individuals tend to have a strong support network in place to help them in times of need. Resilient people don't just shove down their emotions and stoically push forward without support. They lean on their network and draw from the strength and help of others.[12]

Resilience also does not mean the absence of distress or trauma. Resilient people have often experienced significant difficulties in their lives. The key to overcoming or bouncing back following hardship is how you are able to deal with it. Resilient individuals are able to manage those emotions and deal with past trauma in healthy ways. Resilience helps protect against burnout, economic hardship, and demanding jobs, and helps people become more adaptable rather than rigid.[13]

There are various theories on how to build resilience, but most contain elements of the following four categories:

1. Connection. Build your network! Prioritize the relationships in your life, including professional contacts, friends, and family. In addition, consider joining professional associations, religious or spiritual groups, recreational sports teams, or any other group of interest either professionally or socially. The support from these relationships can help provide you with empathy, distraction, a sense of purpose, or even a different perspective in tough times.

2. *Physical Wellness.* Take care of your body to support your mind. Cultivating a healthy lifestyle is key to reducing stress, building energy and stamina, and thinking clearly. Consider making regular exercise, meditation, healthy eating, and proper sleep priorities in life.

3. *Mental Wellness.* Mental health and wellness can be supported through activities such as meditation and visualization, as well as reducing negative self-talk. Keeping a positive outlook on life, being open to change, learning from the past, and seeking help when needed are all key factors.

4. *Meaning.* Find your purpose in life. What is important to you? How do you want to make a difference in the world and what do you want to be remembered for? Having a clear vision of your life's purpose helps keep challenges in perspective, and also provides sources of joy and satisfaction. Consider volunteering or contributing to social issues of interest, mentoring younger colleagues or youth in your community, or joining a community-based charity to strengthen local relationships and give back in a tangible way.[14]

Developing Self-Confidence and Self-Esteem

Just like every other aspect of mental toughness, self-confidence is a skill that can be developed. So often people wish they were confident, but upon further inspection, it becomes obvious that they are doing very little to actually cultivate confidence in their daily lives. They attribute their lack of confidence to outside forces – if they looked better, had more money, had the job of their dreams, or could find a partner – they would be more confident.

This thinking backfires by giving away your personal power to forces out of your control. You don't need money, beauty, or power to be self-confident. You don't need someone else's validation to be confident, and in fact, you should avoid falling into that trap under any circumstances. Rather than making excuses for what isn't, let's focus on taking control and making the right changes to develop the type of self-confidence that contributes to the development of resilience and mental toughness.

1. Start with a strong desire to build confidence. You will find that in many of the steps that follow, mind over matter is a huge part of the process.

2. Fake it till you make it! As we know, thoughts, feelings, and actions influence each other. Then put in the work to build the competence needed to reach your goals.

3. Cultivate your armor. You don't need designer clothes to feel confident, but cultivating the image you present to the world can help you feel in control and help increase your self-confidence. How do you want to show up in the world? It may not mean suits or fancy dress, but consider the image you want to portray, and then begin consciously cultivating it.[15]

4. Control your physical body. How you carry yourself, your posture, facial expressions, and more can help increase your confidence. Discover your personal "power pose" that makes you feel confident and comfortable in your own skin.

5. Exercise your body and your mind. Physical exercise of any kind has a positive effect on our mood and confidence levels. Likewise, meditation is known to help strengthen self-confidence, self-esteem, and resilience.

6. Get specific about your goals and then spend time daily visualizing yourself reaching them.

7. Eliminate negative self-talk and give yourself permission to take risks and make mistakes. Practice self-compassion, and if you fail, then try again.[16] Seek out feedback from those you can trust and surround yourself with people who will support your endeavors.

Action Steps

1. Build your network. Resilience isn't a solitary sport. A strong network of people in different areas of life can provide you with the support you need to be resilient in difficult times. Make a list of people in your network and how they can support you in building resilience. Are there areas where someone is missing? Make a plan to fill those gaps.

2. Visualize success. Visualization is useful for both small challenges and large ones. Spend 5-10 minutes daily visualizing the person you want to be and the image you want to portray. Confident? Competent? Poised? Create the image in your head and spend time daily visualizing yourself interacting with others in a way that projects that image. Is there a big event coming, such as a presentation or an important event? Use your visualization time in the weeks leading up to the event to visualize yourself succeeding in your role.

3. Shut down negative self-talk. Consider using the Three Column Challenge technique to reframe your thoughts. Column one: Write down the negative thoughts. Column two: Identify the cognitive distortion in the statement. Where is it not logical? Column three: Reframe the original thought to be more accurate, rational, or positive. This is not about erasing the truth, but about reframing it in a more productive light.

Self-confidence is a state of mind. While it's not as simple as that sounds to actually develop, with the right approach, anyone can command a room and have the confidence to go for their goals. The challenge now? How to set goals that align with your true vision of how you want your life to be. Stop chasing every opportunity that comes your way and start chasing the ones that align with your real dreams. I'll show you how in Chapter 5.

Chapter Summary

- Self-confidence is the belief and trust you have in yourself and in your ability to face adversity.

- Self-esteem is your feeling of self-worth and self-respect, and is not tied to your skills or abilities.
- Resilience is the ability to successfully adapt to life's challenges and to bounce back from adversity.
- Resilience is a "team sport," built through connection, physical wellness, mental wellness, and finding meaning in life.

5

______

SETTING AND AIMING FOR THE RIGHT TARGETS

HOW CREATING CLEAR, ATTAINABLE, AND
DEADLINE-DRIVEN GOALS CAN HELP STEER
YOUR LIFE IN THE RIGHT DIRECTION

Do you know what you want your life to look like by the end of this year? In five years? Ten? If you don't know which path to choose, life will choose it for you. The old story about climbing the ladder is relevant. You can spend years climbing the ladder, whether at work, in a relationship, or a leisure pursuit, but if you are climbing the wrong ladder, your efforts are wasted.

If your goals aren't perfectly clear and aligned with your authentic self, you will find yourself achieving goals that are not meaningful to you, while watching your real dreams slip away.

Benefits of Goal Setting

Goal setting and monitoring are key to personal and professional growth. Self-awareness means understanding your inner values and motivations, but mindfulness is how we live in a manner that is consistent with those values and motivations. Setting goals and tracking your progress toward reaching them keeps your motivations and values in alignment with your actions. How we spend our days will eventually dictate how we spend our lives.

Mentally tough people are mindful and self-aware, and live their lives with purpose. It is much easier to be consistent, persistent, and resilient when we are facing challenges to them than when we feel lost or out of touch with our inner dreams. When setting goals, it is important that they truly reflect our authentic selves, and are aligned with our values, interests, and needs, rather than influenced by other people or feelings such as guilt or a desire to keep someone else happy.

What does it mean to "be your authentic self?" Essentially it means that you know who you are inside, including your strengths and weaknesses, personality traits, and what you do and don't want from life. It also means that you own those things and take responsibility for them, trusting that you know what's best for you. Finally, it's having the courage to live according to what you know works best for you, and not get caught up in trying to please others.

When we live according to our truest values, in a state of mindfulness, we are more likely to maintain our motivation in our daily lives, have an enhanced sense of well-being, and develop effective coping strategies for stress. Well-planned goals help keep us on the path to self-concordance, or the pursuit of goals that reflect our authentic self.[1] Life's too short to live by someone else's rules!

That all sounds great, but how do I do it?

Have you ever set ambitious goals for yourself and then promptly forgot about them? Or started off strong and then eventually either lost interest or realized that you didn't know how to reach them? If effective goal setting were as easy as putting your goals down on paper and watching them actualize, we would all be living our dream lives.

Successful goal setting and completion are actually more of a science than an art. Some methods work better than others. I have compiled a list below of some of the proven, most-effective techniques for goal-setting and management that are applicable to both individuals, teams, and organizations. Choose the one that you think best suits you, and get planning!

SMART Goals

SMART goals are one of the most popular methods for setting, monitoring, and achieving big goals, and for good reason. Often, people set big goals for themselves, but give up on them because they were unable to create a viable plan for actually achieving them. If your goal is to learn a new language or to run a marathon "someday," those dreams can seem impossible to achieve, and even the most motivated and resilient person can find themselves discouraged to the point of giving up. That's where SMART goals come in.

SMART stands for Specific, Measurable, Achievable, Relevant, and Time-bound.[2] It breaks a big dream into smaller milestones that work like stepping stones to success. The thought of learning a new language or running a marathon at an unidentifiable time in the future may be too vague, but SMART goals take those vague ideas and clarify them to make them achievable.

Specific: Each SMART goal must be really, really specific. In both examples above, the goals are too vague. Which language would you like to learn, to what degree of fluency, and how long will you give yourself to reach the goal? Likewise, running a marathon "someday" isn't specific enough. Choose a date by which you would like to achieve this goal. Is there a particular marathon you would like to qualify for? Changing your goal from "I want to learn a new language" to "I will pass the Beginner Korean exam in eight months" is much more specific. Changing "I want to run a marathon" to "I will train for the local marathon held one year from now" is a more specific goal.

It is often overlooked that in setting SMART goals, a large goal may require multiple smaller milestones. Your larger goal may require multiple units of measurement to be successful. This can help you see exactly which areas are going well and which areas need more attention or even tweaking to keep on track.

Measurable: How are you going to manage your progress? Setting a goal and then not keeping track of progress until the goal is supposed to be achieved is a recipe for disaster. Once the initial excitement of starting something new wears off, measuring milestones can keep you moving forward.

Signing up for a beginner Korean course and enrolling in the beginner exam are great steps. Mapping out the topics you need to cover for the exam and measuring attainment through weekly quizzes is better. Marathon training should involve weekly running goals that can be measured and charted. Likewise, measurable milestones allow for flexibility in reassessing goals regularly rather than all or nothing at the end. If you injure your ankle three months into marathon training, your ongoing milestones will need to be adjusted, or your end goal may need to be reassessed.

Achievable: Dreaming big is great, but your dreams have to be realistic. That doesn't mean dreaming small. It simply means making sure your plan for success is something you can reasonably achieve within the parameters you have set out. A goal of "speaking Korean" within eight months is probably unrealistic for most people with no background in the language. Passing a beginner-level exam is more achievable, and then can be built upon for further fluency.

Setting smaller, more achievable goals that can be used as a foundation for continued growth is preferable to setting one huge goal that quickly becomes overwhelming and is later abandoned.

Relevant: Make sure the milestones are relevant. Sounds like common sense, but sometimes we get caught up in details that aren't important, and they distract us from what is. Have you ever avoided starting a daunting task by doing things like reorganizing your desk? We sometimes do this on purpose, but often without realizing it.

You don't need a special notebook, several textbooks, or the perfect practice partner to start learning Korean. If an in-person class isn't available for the next six months, sign up for something online instead of waiting. Don't get caught up in irrelevant details or milestones. Keep your focus on what's important.

Time-bound: Part of keeping yourself accountable is by having specific milestones and deadlines. In our examples, we have set eight months for writing a beginner Korean exam and one year to train for a marathon, but each milestone also needs to be kept to a schedule. If there are eight chapters to cover for the exam, you must complete one chapter a month to be ready.

Again, flexibility is important. Taking a month off marathon training to heal the ankle you injured three months into your training schedule means that you need to re-evaluate the remaining training schedule to keep on track. If you don't have milestones and a timeline to achieve your goals, you may not realize that you aren't ready to run the marathon until it's too late for course correction.

Remember Mihaela? Her goal was to earn that promotion at the next employee review meeting in six months. If she has cleared her bias, performed a SWOT analysis, and worked on her self-confidence, she has everything in place to adequately identify the milestones she needs to achieve to be ready for that promotion.

<u>OKRs</u>

Objectives and Key Results (OKR), first rolled out in the 1970s, is a framework frequently used in business to define or set an objective, and then the metrics by which the results will be measured. Large organizations such as Google use this method, but it is applicable to smaller teams or even individuals.[3] The basic format is "I/We will ______ as measured by __________."

Let's look at how this works more closely, to see how it can help you achieve your own objectives at work or in your personal life.

Objectives: An objective, simply put, is what you want to achieve. They should be concrete, specific, action-oriented, and significant. You should be thinking big!

Key Results: These are the milestones by which you will judge your ongoing progress. When they are all accomplished, you will have met your objective. They should be specific, timebound, and measurable.

Objectives can be long-term goals, but key objectives should be short-term to be able to gauge progress and keep on track. Objectives are what you want to do, and key results are how you are going to do it. Let's take a closer look at OKRs in action.

Aiden manages a call center team for a national bank. The call center runs monthly competitions, setting goals for all the sales teams to reach monthly targets in areas such as new account openings, investment product signups, and mortgage applications completed, with the results posted on a large whiteboard in a prominent location in the office.

The problem? Aiden supervises the night shift, which traditionally has the lowest number of inbound calls, and outbound cold calls because outbound calls are not allowed during certain hours overnight. Despite this, his team continues to have the same quota objectives as all the others, something they have been struggling to achieve and that has been affecting morale. They currently average 65-75% of the goals and regularly fall in the bottom two of six teams.

This Monday, rather than hold his regular weekly team meeting, he decides to work with his team on setting OKRs to find a way to catch up to, and eventually surpass, the other teams. Rather than focusing on the challenges of being on the night shift, Aiden chooses a different approach. The team works through a series of exercises to analyze the strengths and weaknesses of their own and the others, and to identify the advantages of the night shift. They realized that while their team was falling short, the teams that scored 1st place from month to month rarely exceeded 105% of the monthly goal, and that most teams only achieved 90-95% of the goal. They also realized that while their team never won, there wasn't one team that really had a lock on the competition, meaning that no particular time of day had a definite sales advantage.

When looking at the night shift, they realized that while they had limited time to make outbound calls, the ones they could make, particularly the early morning ones, were markets that were often neglected by the other teams. In addition, the inbound calls generally came in from people already at home and off work, and who were typically able to spend more time on the phone, allowing for a more relaxed sales pitch. Finally, the night shift is 12 hours, compared to the 8-hour morning and afternoon shifts. They all agreed that the extra four hours offered an opportunity for taking their sales to the next level.

Here's what they came up with:

Objective: We will exceed our monthly quotas as measured by achieving 110% of them within three months. We will be the top-performing team as measured by surpassing the other teams within four months.

Key Result 1: Assign 80% of the team to outbound calls during the first two hours of the night shift, before the outbound call time ends, leaving the remaining 20% to handle inbound calls. Repeat during the last two hours of the shift, when the daytime outbound call time begins again. Achieve 85% of the quota by the end of the first month.

Key Result 2: Score no lower than 3rd place in the team competition by the end of the second month.

Key Result 3: Create a lead generator tool for the entire team with clients who show an interest or who requested callbacks, so that any member available can follow up on potential sales, in order to increase sales to 110% of the monthly quota by the end of the third month.

Key Result 4: Be the #1 team in the team competition by the end of the fourth month.

This example shows how the tool works on a team level, but it is also easily applicable to individual goals. The key results are clear, and there is no room for confusion about what constitutes success. The goals are either met or not, and that clarity makes it simple to know what needs to be tweaked moving forward.

WOOPs

Wish, Outcome, Obstacle, Plan (WOOP) is a realistic approach to goal setting and achievement. Unlike SMART goals or OKRs, the WOOP process was created specifically with individuals rather than organizations in mind. It focuses much attention on your own inner obstacles to reaching your dreams, and helps you overcome them.[4]

Wish: This is what you want to accomplish. Choose a goal that is slightly intimidating, but not completely overwhelming. Something you feel would make a big difference in your life, but that you know you need a plan to achieve. A Wish might be to complete an MBA program.

Outcome: In this framework, imagining the outcome goes beyond the goal itself. For example, if your goal is to successfully complete an MBA that will help you switch to your dream career path, the outcome is not just the successful completion of the program. It goes further, to how reaching the desired outcome will change and enhance your life. Completing the program is the bare minimum. Pivoting one step closer to your dream job is the real outcome, and the way that would make you feel and how it would change your life for the better should be the focus.

Obstacles: This goal-planning system differs from others discussed in this chapter because WOOP obstacles are focused internally rather than externally. If you struggle to follow through on goals even when everything is seemingly in place for success, this step may make all the difference. Take the wish of completing an MBA. How do you see yourself potentially sabotaging your efforts to reach this goal? Maybe you have a habit of quitting things halfway through. Perhaps you overbook yourself and end up not being able to give anything your best effort. We all have our inner struggles, and you know yourself best. Identify the factor or factors that are most likely to get in the way of your success.

Plan: This is where you get real about how you are going to overcome that obstacle in order to make your wish come true. What are you going to do differently this time to not get sucked into the same cycle you've seen in the past? If you are worried that you will quit the MBA when the going gets tough, perhaps make the effort to join an online group or an in-person study group to keep you accountable. Though not explicitly a part of the WOOP framework, including details like a timeframe for completion is useful for seeing the light at the end of the tunnel. The more detailed the plan, the better the chance of success!

<u>The Pareto Principle</u>

While not created as a goal-setting framework, the Pareto Principle is an excellent tool for setting priorities and managing your time. This is all about doing less, but getting more from your efforts.

The Pareto Principle stems from the observations of an Italian economist, Vilfredo Pareto. In the late 1800s, he noticed that approximately 20% of the plants in his garden were bearing around 80% of the fruit. Then, in the early 1900s, he noted that about 20% of Italy's population owned approximately 80% of the wealth. He developed the Pareto Distribution, used to describe different types of observable phenomena and proposed that his ratio could be found in many areas in the natural world. The Pareto Principle was coined in the 1940s by Dr. Joseph Juran, who simplified the original idea and applied it to his own area of operations management. It was widely adopted in business circles and later expanded to personal applications.[5]

How? It focuses on which 20% of activities will get you 80% of the results you are looking for. While not a hard and fast ratio, it's the concept of putting your resources where they will have the most impact. The idea here is definitely to work smarter, not harder. It's figuring out where to focus your time, energy, and attention for the most effective results.[6] By considering this ratio in your goal setting, you will be able to create an approach to reaching those goals that is streamlined and that provides the results you're looking for in the most efficient and effective way possible.

Applying this principle to any aspect of your life will help you be more productive overall, and can even be used to eliminate unnecessary items and activities. The Capsule Wardrobe concept is a simple example of the Pareto Principle at work. A Capsule Wardrobe is a small collection of clothing, specifically chosen to maximize the number of outfits while minimizing the number of items.

Think about the clothes you have in your closet right now. How much do you wear regularly, and how much gets worn on occasion, if at all? If you're like many people, you probably wear 20% of your clothes regularly and leave the other 80% to take up space. Whittling down your clothing to the 20% you love and wear means you can save money on clothing, save space in your closet, and save time getting dressed, streamlining your morning routine in the process.

Identifying those tasks and goals that are both important and impactful will help filter out time-consuming tasks that may appear urgent, but ultimately are unimportant to accomplishing your goals.

Personal Mission Statement

Have you ever noticed that large corporations, charities, and other organizations often have a mission statement hanging in a prominent place in their buildings? Something that defines what they are all about, and that keeps them focused as an organization?

Now it's time for you to write yours!

Why a personal mission statement? Just like a corporate mission statement, it helps define the direction in which you want to take your life. It should outline what you stand for, your values, and the direction in which you want to take your life. In short, it describes your "why".[7]

A mission statement is not a long, drawn-out manifesto. To be effective, it should be no more than two to three sentences long. It should embody only the essentials and should be written in positive language. As we know, language matters. A personal mission statement should clearly express what you stand for, rather than giving power to what you don't.

While the statement may be short, it should be powerful. Take some time to first really define who you are, who you would like to become, and the legacy you would like to leave while formulating your personal mission statement.

What or who inspires you? What are the values by which you live your life? What do you stand for? What legacy do I want to leave when I'm gone? Consider brainstorming first, and then whittle down those ideas to the essential until you have a statement that feels right.

Is a mission statement set in stone? It can be, if you are able to adequately capture everything you want and those beliefs don't change over time. However, it's actually a good idea to take the time to come back to your mission statement on at least a yearly basis to make sure it still accurately represents your vision for your life.

A mission statement should be dynamic, not a one-and-done deal! Writing the statement is the first step. Living it is more important. Keeping it in a place where you see it regularly will help both keep you on track and also help you realize if you think it needs updating.

Here are a few examples to get you started:

"To be an agent of positive changes at home, the workplace, and the community at large. I will use my knowledge, talent, and abilities to build a loving family, be the best employee I can be, and help people in need in my community."[8]

"To work on becoming a better version of myself by developing habits and behaviors that align with my core values and belief system. I will be able to create healthy and satisfying relationships within my family, at work, and in the wider community. Success in establishing meaningful and mutually supportive relationships will mean less stress and more happy days."[9]

Persistence

Setting your goals, while hard work, is much easier than actually achieving them. We are often highly motivated during the planning phase and get started full of excitement and optimism, but falter along the road to completion.

Why?

Motivation fills us with adrenaline and is very useful for getting started, but it isn't enough to keep us going. We need discipline, resilience, and persistence to keep moving forward even when we no longer have the same momentum.

Persistence is the ability to continue along a course of action, even when faced with difficulties or obstacles along the way. Attributes include grit, resilience, resolve, and determination. Mentally tough individuals actively cultivate strategies for increasing their ability to persist in the face of adversity.

When pursuing goals, one of the ways to help ensure success is to not only frame really clear goals but to also break those goals down into small, achievable milestones. Then keep motivation high by celebrating each of those small wins!

Build in accountability checks and consider finding accountability partners from your personal life or online accountability groups to provide support along your journey. It is important to remind yourself of your why, so keeping prominently placed reminders of how your life will change when you reach your goals can help keep you on track.

While none of us can predict the future, we can certainly put in place the mechanisms to take control of the present in order to orient our lives in the direction we want the future to take. Make no mistake, pursuing your goals is not easy. How do you handle your own emotions and stress levels when things get tough? In Chapter 6, I give you the blueprint for emotional regulation and stress management that you put to work for you immediately.

Action Steps

1. Get clear on what you want. Before choosing which goal-setting method is best for you, you must first have goals to set! There are several ways to help get clear on what you want. Consider brainstorming, list making, journaling, or take a visual approach and create a vision board with photos or other visuals that represent the life you want to cultivate.

2. Choose your method and get goal-setting. Whether you prefer SMART goals, OKRs, or WOOPs, choose a method and start getting your goals down where you can easily access them and track your ongoing progress. Whether you prefer to use pen and paper, an online spreadsheet, or an app for this specific purpose, the important thing is to get the goals out of your head and somewhere concrete.

3. Write your personal mission statement. A well-written statement serves almost like your north star, keeping you motivated and on track through good times and bad. Take the time to really focus on this, and then place it somewhere you will see it regularly.

Key Takeaways

- Effective goal setting is the secret weapon to achieving your dreams. They increase motivation and focus, provide a sense of direction, and help you persist in following through.
- SMART Goals are goals that are Specific, Measurable, Achievable, Relevant, and Time-bound.
- OKR is a goal-setting system often found in the world of business. It stands for Objectives and Key Results, and helps individuals and teams focus on their most important objectives, while providing a measurement tool to gauge success rates.
- WOOP stands for Wish, Outcome, Obstacle, and Plan. First, identify a wish or goal. Second, imagine the desired outcome of said wish. Third, identify potential obstacles to reaching the goal. Fourth, design a plan to overcome those obstacles and achieve success.
- The Pareto Principle is all about laser focus. Focus on the 20% of the action that will yield 80% of the results.

- Write a Personal Mission Statement of your purpose and values. It provides a compass by which goals and decisions should be aligned.
- Cultivate persistence. Develop strategies to stay on track, such as strong goal setting, breaking goals into measurable chunks, celebrating small wins to keep morale up, and finding accountability partners to greatly enhance the chances of success.

6

MASTERING YOUR EMOTIONS

WHY ACKNOWLEDGING AND MANAGING YOUR EMOTIONS IS CRUCIAL TO BECOME MENTALLY TOUGH

Airports are stressful places. Everyone there has their own agenda of where they want to go, but almost no control over the process of getting there. What you can bring, how much of it, which documents you need to be allowed on the flight, and whether the flight itself even leaves on time are just some of the factors outside the control of the average passenger. Add to that the line-ups, the waiting, and the crowds in general, and it adds up to an emotional, stressful situation under the best of circumstances. And when something goes wrong, like a delayed or canceled flight? It can be a recipe for disaster.

Have you ever watched someone lose it at the airport? Yelling, threatening, accusing airline staff at the top of their lungs? Stomping around, making phone call after phone call, and complaining loudly to anyone who will listen? Even if they are justified in their frustration, desperation, and anger, their behavior can be so off-

95

putting that nobody wants to associate with them because they seem so volatile. And their stress level? Through the roof! You can see it rise as they get more and more upset.

The worst part? They are often reacting to a genuinely infuriating situation, but in a manner that is not conducive to getting the results they want. In many cases, little can be done in the moment. Front-line staff can't make a delayed flight leave earlier and they aren't the ones who decide to cancel a flight. All those negative emotions spilling out are being directed ineffectively in the wrong direction, and in the worst possible manner for all involved.

Should people not get angry and frustrated when bad things happen? Of course not! We can't necessarily control the emotions that pop up. What we can control is how we manage them. Do we stew over something for days or talk it out? Do we blow up when inconvenienced or try to find a calm way to express our frustration? How we handle our emotions is key to building mental toughness. The same applies to stress. Stressful situations and people are inevitable. Letting the stress consume us is not.

Fortunately, controlling our emotions and changing how we handle stress is completely within our control, and this chapter will introduce you to the techniques that are sure to change your relationship to both.

Negative Emotions

Most of us are fairly skilled at managing positive emotions like joy, and few people complain about their easygoing spouse or colleague. However, emotions that are considered "negative emotions" can be harder to get under control. Emotions such as anger, fear, jealousy, anxiety, shame, hatred, or even sadness can impair our ability to think rationally and can result in poor decisions or detrimental behavior. If we can learn to use these emotions to serve us rather than to work against us, we improve our mental toughness and can turn a negative into a positive asset.

The truth is, there really aren't any "negative emotions" in the sense that emotions in and of themselves are not negative. At their core, emotions are kinds of sensors telling you to pay more attention to a person, place, thing, or event. It's often easier for us to recognize those factors when the emotion is "good" because such feelings leave us wanting more. We seek out the people or activities that make us happy. The ones that keep us laughing, smiling, or generally just feeling positive about ourselves.

Negative emotions are more complicated because they are often feelings we wish to avoid. However, these emotions can be incredibly useful if we are able to analyze them objectively, and then take action to minimize them in the future.

Take fear, for example. Being afraid in certain situations is an emotion that can literally save your life. Jealousy often makes us aware of wants that we didn't previously know we had. Shame can be an excellent deterrent to repeating an action that isn't in our best interests. Anger can alert us to our triggers, or help us avoid similar people or situations in the future.

So, if they're so useful, what makes these emotions negative?

The damage they can do to our mental health and well-being when we dwell on the emotion, without doing the work to change the situation or avoid it in the future. Dwelling on negative emotions also increases stress levels, and a failure to manage stress effectively can negatively impact our physical and mental health, which may affect every aspect of our lives.

Learning to acknowledge the emotion, accept it as valid, process and manage it, and learn from it before releasing it and pivoting toward more positive emotions is how mentally tough people with high Emotional Intelligence, or EQ, handle negative emotions in a productive manner.

Emotional Quotient

EQ is one's ability to identify, assess, and manage their own emotions, as well as to recognize and positively influence the emotions of others. EQ encompasses five domains, covering both internal and external factors.[1]

1. <u>Self-Awareness</u>: As discussed in previous chapters, self-awareness includes the ability to accurately assess your strengths and weaknesses. It also encompasses your self-esteem and your awareness of your own emotions. You must first be able to accurately identify what you are feeling and why before you can work to regulate and control them.

2. <u>Self-Regulation:</u> This is where your self-control comes into play. You may be angry, but you are responsible for your response. You can choose to scream, punch a wall, start a fight… or not. You can also choose to walk away entirely or decide to pause an argument and come back to it when you are calmer. When you are able to self-regulate, you are more conscientious, adaptable, and trustworthy.

3. <u>Self-Motivation</u>: When you have a high EQ, you are able to make your emotions work for you. Jealous of your coworker's promotion? Channel it into motivation to do better yourself. Self-motivated people have a drive that comes from within, the initiative to start, and the commitment to see things through.

4. <u>Social Awareness</u>: This domain looks outward. You become aware of the needs of others and use emotions like empathy to inform your engagement in the big areas of service activities, diversity inclusion, or political engagement, as well as the smaller, everyday applications such as being a good listener or mediating conflicts at work or in your personal life. Being socially aware helps

you better understand where your skills can be used in the service of others.

5. <u>Social Skills</u>: People with high EQs understand the importance of developing social skills in order to make the most impact in all types of relationships. Strong leaders know how to communicate and influence others on their team. In personal relationships, being able to empathize and control your emotions during arguments or personal conflicts can help solve problems while preserving the integrity of the relationships that are important to you.[2]

Stress Management

The World Health Organization defines stress as a "state of worry or mental tension caused by a difficult situation. Stress is a natural human response that prompts us to address challenges and threats in our lives."[3] Stress is something that everyone experiences throughout their lives, and while a little bit of stress isn't harmful, excessive amounts of stress that are not well-managed are harmful to our physical and emotional well-being.

Stress can make us irritable or angry, make it difficult to relax, affect our appetite or ability to fall asleep at night, or increase our anxiety. Physically it can result in sore muscles, aches and pains, or upset stomach. It can exacerbate existing mental health conditions as well.[4]

Since eliminating stress entirely is not realistic, how can we learn to keep it in check? By putting in place any number of Stress Management Interventions, or SMIs. SMIs have been shown to increase work performance, improve relationships, and reduce sickness and absenteeism in the workplace.[5] The effects extend to all areas of life. People who are less stressed are better able to enjoy life in general.

While some stress is beneficial, too much stress is dangerous to our health. Before trying to manage stress, we should proactively look for ways to minimize unnecessary stress. This is where a self-audit of the stressors in your life is useful.

Which situations cause you the most stress? Are they all completely out of your control, or are there ways to relieve some of the stress? What can be delegated or outsourced? If housework or cooking has become a source of stress in your relationship, is hiring someone to clean or ordering from a meal service an option? Thinking outside the box and removing or lessening as many stressors as possible is the first step in stress management.

Now it's time to implement stress management techniques for the stressors that remain. Mentally strong people are resilient and can push through stress, but truly mentally strong people handle stress through the use of management techniques. We can't always control what life throws at us, but we can control how we respond to it.

<u>Self-regulation Techniques</u>

Self-regulation techniques work to keep you calm in the face of the proverbial storm by helping you learn to control your physical responses to stress. How does your body react when stressed? Do your shoulders hunch and does your breathing get shallow? Do your muscles clench? Progressive muscle relaxation, where you tense muscles individually and then relax them one by one, can help your body let go of the physical tension that often accompanies stressful situations.[6]

When starting progressive relaxation, it can be helpful to use a guided audio or to take a class. This is an excellent activity to do before bed if you find it hard to relax. If you want to give it a try on your own, consider the following steps:

1. Find a quiet place to lie down, free of distractions, and get in a comfortable position.

2. Close your eyes, and take a few calming breaths.

3. Starting at your toes, curl them under and hold them tightly for 10-15 seconds, then let them go. Repeat the process with your calves, and thighs, working your way up your body. Don't forget the muscles of the face!

4. Take a few more calming breaths before opening your eyes, or better yet, before drifting off to sleep!

Deep breathing exercises can reel in both a racing heart and a racing mind by lowering your heart rate, clearing your thoughts, and bringing your breathing into calm focus. Meditation, even for a few minutes a day, can help release tension and anxiety, calm the mind and body, and give you the clarity you need to handle stress without getting overwhelmed.

Journaling is a way to get those negative emotions and stressors out of your mind and onto paper where they can then be examined more objectively. Likewise, speaking to a friend about a particularly distressing issue can help you see things from a different perspective.

Expert Help

Don't hesitate to look to the experts for help if you need it. Being mentally tough doesn't mean you have to go it alone. It means that you know when to ask for help. Consider mindfulness training, resilience training, coping skills training, or even cognitive behavioral therapy to help keep the negative effects of emotional dysregulation and stress at bay.

Physical Exercise

Exercise should not be overlooked. The benefits of exercise on the body are well-documented, but not everyone realizes just how good physical exercise is for the mind. A mix of different types of exercise is ideal. Cardiovascular exercise strengthens the heart and clears the mind. Strength training improves discipline. Yoga, tai chi, or martial arts are mind-body activities that help lower stress and improve emotional control and self-regulation.

Visualization

Visualization, or mental imagery, is when we form a mental picture of something. When using visualization for emotional regulation, stress reduction, or goal achievement, visualization goes beyond the creation of a static image. It is creating an image in your mind of exactly how you would like something to happen.

Does the idea that by simply thinking about something you can change your circumstances in reality sound too good to be true? It's not, and there's science to back it up! Visualization has been used as a healing practice for hundreds of years and has been proven to help reduce pain and other symptoms of illness.[7]

Athletes have also been using visualization to help them improve performance for decades. They often use visualizations of entire performances, such as mentally going through a ski run, before performing the activity. Mental practice has been shown to be almost as effective as physical practice on muscles as thoughts have been shown to have almost the same effect on the brain as physically moving the muscles themselves. Visualization enhances the mind-body connection in positive ways.[8]

In developing mental toughness, visualization can help manage stress and anxiety. It can also help with goal setting and achievement.

One of the simplest uses of visualization is what is known as the palming technique. Place the palms of your hands over your eyes and imagine the color you associate with stress. Then imagine switching the color to one you associate with calmness and relaxation.[9] Sounds simple, but it works! This is an easy visualization activity that can be done almost anywhere, at any time, and that takes only a minute or two to complete.

More complex visualization techniques can be used for more difficult situations, or to help you feel prepared and more relaxed before a stressful event or activity. Does public speaking cause you anxiety? Visualize the entire speech-giving experience to help reduce your anxiety. When visualizing, try to use all of your senses.

Let's look at the example of public speaking in more detail. Imagine you are giving an important presentation to a room of 50 people. Your visualization should begin before the actual public speaking part begins, and the entire process should be imagined as though it is happening in the moment, or has already successfully taken place. What are you wearing? What is the weather like? Is it very hot outside but cool and air-conditioned in the presentation room? Do you have a glass of cool water to sip on as you speak? Where will you stand?

Now think about the presentation itself. Imagine facing the audience and taking a few calming breaths before you start. Now imagine yourself going through the presentation in as much detail as possible. You nail the presentation! You are now speaking one-on-one to some of those present, and everyone is congratulating you on the great job you've done.

We have already talked about how your thoughts can affect your emotions, and visualization is one way to help train your mind to perform a certain way long before you perform in that scenario.

There are a variety of ways to use this technique to create those positive connections in your brain. Start with guided meditations that are already created to help you get an idea of how it works, and to help with general things like reducing anger or letting go of frustration.

Action Steps

1. *Build your Emotional Quotient (EQ).* If you have never thought about your EQ before, start at the beginning by observing and naming your emotions. Being aware of how you feel in different situations and accurately naming them is the first step to building self-awareness, the first element of EQ.

2. *Do a stress audit.* Make a list of the stressors in your life and categorize them in a way that makes sense to you. Go through each item individually and see which can be eliminated, which can be minimized, and which will need to be managed. Then make a plan to tackle them!

For example, if cutting the lawn weekly is a stressor, hiring someone to cut it can eliminate the stress. Sharing responsibility for cutting it with another person can minimize it. Rewarding yourself after cutting the lawn yourself can manage it.

3. Get moving! If you don't already have a regular exercise routine in place, now is the time to start. The mind-body connection is strong, and exercise is not just good for your body, but also for what ails you emotionally. It doesn't have to be perfect. It just needs to get you moving.

Already active? Where could you change things up for the most impact? Maybe you enjoy a mix of cardio and strength training, but could benefit from an activity that encourages more flexibility, like yoga or functional movement training.

3. Practice color breathing. This is an excellent introduction to visualization that builds on the palming technique introduced earlier in the chapter. This technique can be used to help with managing emotions and reducing stress. Think of how you currently feel. Assign that emotion a color. Now think of how you want to feel. Assign that emotion a color. Breathe deeply and slowly while imagining switching the color of how you currently feel to the color you want to feel. With each inhale, imagine the desired color entering your lungs and spreading throughout your body. On each exhale, imagine the color you no longer want leaving your body.

Mastering your emotions, particularly those that can negatively distort your judgment and decision-making skills, allows you to control your thoughts, speech, and behavior. Managing stress allows you to mitigate the negative impact of stress on your mind and body. Now let's learn how to build the positive habits that will serve you for life.

Key Takeaways

- Mastering your emotions and successfully managing stress are crucial to developing and maintaining mental toughness.
- Developing a strong Emotional Quotient (EQ) and implementing stress management techniques are important.
- Negative emotions such as fear, anger, anxiety, and stress can put a drain on mental toughness and impair our ability to think clearly and make rational decisions.
- Emotion and stress management techniques include self-regulation activities such as meditation, breathing techniques, progress muscle regulation, and visualization. Coping mechanisms such as journaling, therapy, hobbies, and cultivating strong friendships are also helpful.
- Physical exercise is a triple threat, helping regulate emotions, manage stress, and increase mental toughness. A combination of cardiovascular exercises, strength training, and mind-body exercises, such as yoga and tai chi, is recommended.
- Visualization is truly an example of mind over matter, training your brain to react how you want in almost any situation by creating the scenario in your mind before you experience it in real life.

7

THE INFLUENCE OF PRODUCTIVE HABITS

HOW YOUR HABITS BECOME THE STEPPING STONES TO BUILDING MENTAL TOUGHNESS

The Merriam-Webster dictionary defines a "habit" as a "settled tendency or usual manner of behavior."[1] The accompanying example is simple enough, the habit of taking a morning walk. This brings to mind the everyday habits that make up a daily routine, like brushing our teeth or washing our faces before bed. They sound simple and almost inconsequential, and yet it is exactly these types of activities that shape our lives. They become automatic parts of our day that we often don't think much about.

If we aren't mindful about exactly which habits we cultivate, we can easily fall into the trap of incorporating negative habits into our lives without realizing it. With the exception of the types of habits that are overtly destructive, such as addiction or self-harm, most habits may seem fairly innocuous until we look at them more closely and with intention. Scrolling online until 3 a.m.

every night might not seem harmful, until you consider the effect of lack of sleep on your overall well-being.

When we think about habit formation with mental toughness in mind, it becomes clear that we need to intentionally cultivate good habits, and prune away bad habits in the same manner. The American Psychological Association's definition of "habit" is more in line with building habits for this purpose: "A well-learned behavior or automatic sequence of behaviors that is relatively situation specific and over time has become motorically reflexive and independent of motivational or cognitive influence—that is, it is performed with little or no conscious intent."[2]

Before we can rely on the force of habit to help us create the life we want, we need to first create those positive habits and eliminate ones that don't serve us. But making healthy habits isn't as simple as deciding you're now going to turn out the lights at 11 p.m. instead of 3 a.m. Positive habits are not typically formed out of sheer willpower alone. If it were that easy, everyone would be living their best life!

So how do we break negative habits and replace them with the kind of positive habits that will support the growth we are seeking to cultivate? This chapter will walk you through the science of breaking bad habits and building good ones and help you develop a plan to make those new habits stick.

Why Positive Habits Are Key to Building Mental Toughness

Building positive habits doesn't happen overnight, like many of the other traits of mental toughness discussed in this book. It is a bit ironic that while the end goal of habit formation is for the action to become automatic, getting to that point requires a lot of intentional planning and practice.

However, habits are a key component of developing mental toughness, as well as developing impulse control and grit. The important thing to remember when working on positive habit formation is that while progress is often incremental, those small steps eventually become big changes.[3] Sticking to the process is where the real work lies.

Building positive habits is associated with many of the benefits we have come to learn as essential components of mental toughness, including enhanced self-esteem and an increased ability to cope with stress. However, perhaps the biggest benefit is that habits require less mental effort, thereby conserving our mental energy for other activities.

Let me explain. When forming habits, we initially need to make a conscious choice to pursue the habit and then perform the action repeatedly. The need to decide every time we act can be mentally draining, particularly when the action we want to take requires some form of sacrifice or delayed gratification.

Let's say you want to be more physically active, but don't have the habit of going to the gym. Every morning you wake up and think about going to the gym that day. Without a habit, you are likely to think about if you feel like going or if there is something else you would rather be doing instead. Following through on your goal of being more physically active becomes subject to your motivation each day. Having to make that decision each day can be mentally and emotionally taxing, making it easier to eventually abandon the new habit altogether.

When you cultivate the habit of going to the gym every Tuesday, Thursday, and Saturday morning, you no longer have to decide whether or not you are going. You aren't relying on your level of motivation, whether you feel like going or any other factor. You are free from having to decide, because the choice was made when you adopted the habit. Freedom from decision-making is a key benefit of positive habits.[4]

This isn't just based on assumption. Neuro-imaging studies have shown that once a behavior becomes automatic, a habit, the action becomes regulated by a different part of the brain associated with less mental effort. In other words, we use fewer mental resources when executing a habit than an action that has not yet been fully adopted as a habit. This, in turn, frees up more mental space and energy for other activities.[5]

How Will I Know Which Habits Are Productive and Which Are Not?

Trying to implement new, positive habits without first addressing the negative habit that is going to be replaced is a recipe for failure. Changing your bedtime to 11 p.m. instead of 3 a.m. and turning off electronics an hour before bed are solid habits to pursue, but they don't address the underlying issues.

What are you getting out of staying up late to scroll social media? Is late at night the only time the house is quiet and you get some time alone, uninterrupted? Is scrolling social media a way to distract your mind from anxious or upsetting thoughts? Until you identify what payoff you are getting from the negative habit and deal with the underlying reasons for that behavior, simply trying to replace it with a more positive habit is unlikely to work over the long term.

First, we must become conscious of the habit in order to take steps to break it. Sounds obvious, but since habits are actually activities we do without thinking, we may not always be as aware of them as we could be. It is easy to underestimate the frequency with which we engage in a negative habit, such as how many hours we spend scrolling social media or how many cigarettes we really smoke when we only "smoke socially." Identifying these habits and then becoming aware of their frequency is a step that shouldn't be skipped.

We may become aware of these habits by relating them to the new positive habit we want to start. If we want to go to bed at 11 p.m. in order to get eight hours of sleep a night, we can keep track of our sleep and wake times for a week or two to fully understand how far off we are from that goal. Similarly, if we want a better picture of where all our money goes each month, creating a proper budgeting spreadsheet and filling it in faithfully for a month can show us where we spend every cent.

Second, figure out the reason behind the behavior and the need it is filling. As mentioned earlier, are you staying up until 3 a.m. because you really can't fall asleep earlier, or because you are craving some alone time and late evening is the only time you have been able to carve out for yourself? Once you have a better sense of the practical and emotional needs these negative habits are filling, you can start looking for more positive habits to replace them.

What might that process look like? Perhaps in the case above of feeling as though late nights are the only alone time you might have, you might start with actually keeping track of how you spend your time from the moment you wake up until you go to sleep for a week. Are there missed opportunities for finding the time you crave? If you're a parent, could you pick the children up from daycare a half hour later? Or would it be better to get up an hour earlier in the morning to start your day uninterrupted?

While some negative habits may not feel terrible in the moment, they ultimately detract from our ability to develop mental toughness and to grow into the best versions of ourselves for two main reasons.

1. Self-destructive behavior catches up to you eventually.

Negative habits may feel good in the moment, but ultimately they stand in the way of our personal growth and maybe even our long-term physical and mental health. Doing something that brings short-term satisfaction but sacrifices long-term well-being does more harm than good and you will eventually have to deal with the consequences, whether small or large.

2. Negative habits are not conducive to building perseverance, grit, or determination.

Why? Because they are often the easier thing to do, not the best thing to do. It takes more effort to start and stick to a budget than to spend now and deal with it later or to stick to an exercise program rather than work out only when you feel like it. When starting a positive habit, we are simultaneously fighting against the ingrained negative habit and the emotional payoff that comes from it in the short term for what are often long-term rewards that aren't immediately available to us. We need to use the components of mental toughness, such as perseverance, grit, and determination to successfully build a positive habit until it becomes automatic.

As we discussed in Chapter 2, grit proves to be more important to success in a number of areas amongst West

Point Military Cadets than superior intellect or physical endowment on surviving the first six weeks and in graduating from the four-year program. Avoiding dealing with the real issues behind your negative habits is a missed opportunity to build grit.

Breaking Bad (Habits, that is)

Unfortunately, breaking bad habits and forming new, positive ones isn't as easy as knowing that the behavior needs changing. Many large-scale health campaigns have successfully raised awareness and managed to change the behavior of their target population temporarily, but the effects tend to be short-lived. A lack of willpower is often blamed for lapses in changed habits, but is only one aspect of why old habits are hard to break and new ones are hard to build.[6]

Habits develop as context-response associations in our memory, in which behavior becomes a habit as we repeat it over and over. Often, people make the mistake of trying to replace the negative behavior with a new, positive habit, assuming that the old habit will be broken as a result. This is not typically as successful as working on breaking the old habit as well as building a new one.

Habits are typically triggered by cues. We might always floss our teeth immediately after brushing them, or grab a cookie when we pour ourselves a cup of tea. Changing or eliminating those context cues helps disrupt the automatic nature of the habit in our brains, thereby disrupting the automatic behavior.

Sometimes disrupting cues involves environmental avoidance or re-engineering. If you go to the casino every Friday night and are unable to stop overspending while there, you may have to stop going entirely to break the habit and find something else to do on a Friday night. This technique is often put in place with recovering alcoholics, in which they not only avoid frequenting the places where they typically overindulge in alcohol but also sometimes must avoid the people with whom they would drink the most in order to minimize temptation.

Unfortunately, we can't always completely avoid the locations that trigger our habits. Our negative habits often occur in places and with people that are part of our daily routines. It's not always feasible to completely avoid these cues, as moving out of your home or quitting your job aren't typically realistic. Instead, try and re-engineer how you function in those spaces to cut the trigger that cues the behavior.

If watching TV at night means consuming a day's worth of calories as a snack, consider reading a book, playing a game, or going for a walk instead. Avoid stocking the fridge and cupboards with foods you can't turn down. The idea is to make engaging with negative habits more difficult in order to eliminate or at least minimize their occurrence.

Monitoring your progress and having a plan for when setbacks occur can also improve your chances of success. Monitoring helps us to have a true vision of how we are doing and minimizes the chances of overreacting or giving up when a setback occurs.[7]

Turning a Negative into a Positive

Rather than completely extinguishing a negative habit before implementing a new positive one, the process is one of change, gradually replacing unwanted behaviors with new ones. This is why the two processes are intertwined. Ideally, when disrupting the negative context cues to break a habit, positive context cues will replace them in order to strengthen the behaviors of the new, desired habits.

Consider tacking on a new habit to another, already successful habit. This is called piggybacking. For example, if you wash your face every morning without fail, consider adding sunscreen to that routine to piggyback on an already positive habit.[8]

While this is a simple action to add to your routine, the process is helpful even for more difficult habits to form. Let's say you really want to eat healthier and start moving more, achieving those ubiquitous 10,000 steps daily. You've started bringing your lunch to work daily, focusing on healthy meals. You can piggyback on that healthy habit by taking a walk as soon as you are finished eating. You may need to start by splitting up your lunch break with a timer at first, such as 30 minutes to eat, followed by a 20-minute walk and 10 minutes to rest before getting back to work.

Avoid choosing new habits that have a finish line, meaning there is a defined natural endpoint to the habit that will require either a renewal or reset at a designated point in the future. Instead, choose open-ended habits that contribute to well-being in a long-term way. A defined goal might be to lose 30 pounds. Then what?

This is one of the reasons why people often cycle through weight gain and loss, when they reach a goal and then return to old habits. A better habit may be to live a healthy lifestyle. Healthy living may mean achieving and maintaining a healthy weight for your body, getting enough sleep, and exercising a certain amount weekly. These are all habits that can positively contribute to your quality of life for many years to come.

Goals vs Values

Setting clear goals, as we saw in <u>Chapter 5</u>, is an important part of orienting our lives in the direction we want. We write those goals ideally based on the values we hold. Wanting to be a good partner is a value. Setting a goal of going out on a date once a week is a goal that is aligned with those values. However, goals can sometimes have a starting and ending point, as mentioned above. A goal might be to save 10% for a downpayment on a house. Once that money is saved, the goal has been reached. The value of that goal might be financial security for you and your family.

Aligning our habits with our overarching values is better than aligning them specifically with a goal. Values are lifelong and provide a long-term incentive to keep going. Additionally, when we align our habits with our values, we often find that we are encouraged to add additional positive habits to our daily routine to further strengthen our commitment to those values.[9]

<u>Lack of accountability is where good intentions go to die</u>

How often have you wanted to do something, planned to do something, or even started to do something, and then somehow it all fell apart? You probably neglected to factor in accountability measures to keep you on track. Accountability requires follow-up and follow-through and makes sure that there is something other than willpower and good intentions to see us through our big ideas.

Accountability measures are often factored into our jobs, and even our relationships, as there is someone or something external to hold us to our promises. But habits are internal and very, very personal. Most of the time, failing to break an old habit or develop a new one hurts us more than anyone, at least in the short term. So how do we hold ourselves accountable?

- Take ownership of your goal. If you don't take promises you make to yourself as important as those you make to others, no other measure of accountability will be a success.

- Keep the behaviors you want to turn into habits top of mind. Write down your actions for the day every morning until those behaviors become a habit. Consider an accountability partner. An accountability partner helps keep you on track, and you do the same for them. You provide each other feedback, work through failures, and celebrate successes together.

Action Steps

1. Identify Negative Habits. Choose one or two negative habits and track them over the course of two weeks. Whenever you engage in the habit, write down as much information as you can to get a better picture of what is driving the behavior. Include information such as where you are, who you are with, and what you felt at the time. Analyze the results to see if you can pinpoint the underlying reasons for the behavior and the reward you are getting from it.

2. Break free. Choose one of the strategies discussed in the chapter and make a plan for tackling the negative habit. Consider:

- Avoiding the triggers
- Re-engineering how you interact with people or places you cannot avoid

- Identify how the habit does not align with your values and which positive habit could replace it that does align

Unlike some of the other action items in the book, there is no set timeline for successfully breaking bad habits. Depending on the habit you choose and its role in your life, breaking it could be relatively easy and painless or something that takes many months to accomplish. Remember that setbacks are normal, and develop strategies for staying motivated throughout the process.

3. *Positive progress.* Choose a new habit you would like to build. Consider your personal life goals and mission statement from <u>Chapter 5</u> when deciding, as your habits can help you reach those goals. Create a daily schedule, accountability techniques, and a tracking method to help increase your chances of success. Fortunately, building new habits is often easier than breaking old ones!

Chapter Summary

- Habits are routine behaviors that have become reflexive and performed with little conscious intent.
- Developing positive habits has a significant impact on building mental toughness.
- It is essential to first identify the negative habits that are impeding our personal growth and

decipher the underlying reasons behind the
behavior.

- Developing positive habits is key to building
  mental toughness and continuing to develop as a
  person.

8

MINDFULNESS MEDITATION

HOW PRACTICING THESE MENTAL EXERCISES CAN BE NECESSARY TOOLS FOR YOUR QUEST TO BECOME MENTALLY TOUGH

Picture yourself at a mountain retreat, looking out over the landscape in a state of internal peace. Your mornings are spent meditating, and your afternoons are dedicated to yoga and silent contemplation.

No? Does the idea of a silent retreat sound great but not realistic? Or maybe the thought of spending hours in silent meditation sounds like torture.

Do practices like mindfulness and meditation sound like the kinds of things you don't have time for and are a waste of time anyway? You're not alone. But, you're also wrong!

While mindfulness and meditation may conjure images of Buddhist monks, it is by no means relegated to the realm of religion and spirituality. Many successful entrepreneurs and business people swear by it as one of the key foundations of their success. Tim Ferris, Ariana

Huffington, Oprah Winfrey, and Jack Dorsey are just a few successful individuals who make the time daily despite their packed schedules to meditate.[1]

Meditation and mindfulness practices are free, simple, and available to all. We may not be able to afford all of the luxuries of the people named above, but we don't need anything fancy or expensive to practice mindfulness and commit to a meditation practice. I'll show you how easy it can be to implement a practice that is almost guaranteed to positively impact your life and help you build mental toughness in just a few minutes a day.

What is mindfulness?

The practice of mindfulness is not new, but it has only recently entered the mainstream as something that can benefit everyone from young children to adults. Mindfulness is being aware of and focusing on the present moment. It involves being aware of your thoughts, feelings, and bodily sensations and observing them without judgment. It is used as a form of therapy to help with stress relief, psychological well-being, symptoms of chronic illness, and emotional regulation, among others.[2]

What is meditation?

It's impossible to talk about mindfulness without diving into the topic of meditation, as they go hand-in-hand. Meditation is an umbrella term for a number of practices. However, four types are most commonly researched: Focused Attention, Open Awareness/Monitoring, Loving

Kindness/Compassion, and Mantra/Transcendental. Research on meditation is complex as different types of meditation have different goals, and neuroscientific research has shown that different areas of the brain are activated or deactivated during different types of meditative states, which we will discuss in more detail later in the chapter.[3]

Choosing any form of meditation can have positive benefits, but we will focus on the first two, Focused Attention and Open Awareness/Monitoring.

Focused Attention meditation involves bringing attention to a particular object of focus and keeping it there. It involves three aspects: 1- Orienting, or bringing attention to the object; 2- Alerting, or detecting targets outside one's usual focus of attention; and 3- Conflict Monitoring, or being able to prioritize among conflicting stimuli.

Open Awareness/Monitoring meditation is the practice of observing all stimuli as they occur without continuing to pay attention to them in either thought or action. We learn to observe and then let go.[4]

Both meditative practices are useful for building mental toughness. They can help improve our ability to hold attention over time, allowing us to build determination, perseverance, and grit. Meditation can also alter our perception, which is heavily influenced by what we pay attention to and expect to see. The more we can intentionally decide which stimuli to pay attention to and in what way, the clearer and more intense our perception becomes.[5]

Mindfulness + Meditation = Mindfulness Meditation

In recent years, mindfulness meditation has become a general term for meditation in general. Specifically, if mindfulness is the ability to be fully aware of the present moment, meditation is the technique that helps us to get there.[6] The goal is to practice mindfulness during meditation so that we can then become mindful at all times, even when not in meditative practice.[7] Mindfulness and meditation are currently popular topics in various areas of study such as psychology, neuroscience, psychiatry, and medicine, to better understand the mind-body connection it elicits.[8]

Mindfulness meditation is a combination of attention and acceptance. Attention focuses on the present moment, often bringing awareness to breath, physical state, thoughts, and emotions. The acceptance aspect is the ability to observe the things that are the objects of your attention without judgment, and then to be able to let them go.[9] Mindfulness meditation techniques can be used by individuals, or as a part of therapy. The central components include the development of attentional skills, emotional regulation, and improved thinking patterns.[10]

There are two main mindfulness meditation interventions, Mindfulness-Based Stress Reduction (MBSR), and Mindfulness-Based Cognitive Therapy

(MBCT). MBSR is typically an eight-week program that combines in-person classes as well as mindfulness activities to do at home. A combination of yoga and meditation is common. MBCT combines elements of Mindfulness-Based Stress Reduction and Cognitive Behavioral Therapy to treat individuals with depression, helping people be less likely to react with negative thoughts or reactions when in stressful periods. They become better able to focus on the present and are less likely to ruminate.[11]

Where's the Science?

Still skeptical of the real-life benefits of mindfulness meditation? Do you believe that testimonials are nice but hard science is better? I've got you covered!

Scientists have studied how the brain changes during meditation, and functional neuroimaging provides a look into the neural processes that are associated with mindfulness. Research suggests that mindfulness meditation affects the functioning of the medial cortex, the associated default network, as well as the insula and amygdala. In addition, changes in the hippocampus have been observed. Meditation changes the brain on a physically observable level, for the better. It stimulates the areas of the brain responsible for attention, automatic thoughts and self-referential thinking, and emotional regulation.[12]

Working Memory

Studies have shown that mindfulness meditation can also positively affect working memory. Working memory is an executive function skill. Short-term memory that is needed for certain cognitive tasks such as problem-solving. One study measured the effect of mindfulness training practice on the working memory of pre-deployment military personnel in the United States Marines during that very stressful period.

Two cohorts were recruited for the study. One cohort, the Military Control (MC) group received no mindfulness training. The other cohort received an eight-week mindfulness training course and then kept track of time spent on formal mindfulness practices outside of the course, on their own time. A third civilian control group with no training was also tested.

Working memory was tested at the beginning of the study, and then nine to ten weeks later. The results were telling. In the civilian cohort, working memory remained stable. However, working memory declined in the military control group, and also decreased for members of the mindfulness training group who spent little out-of-class practice time on formal mindfulness activities. High-stress situations where emotional regulation is a challenge tend to have a negative impact on working memory.

This is why the findings of the military cohort who received mindfulness training and who then continued to practice mindfulness outside of that training are so fascinating. In that group, their working memory actually increased over the course of the study, despite the highly stressful situation they were facing pre-deployment. Simply put, the more you practice mindfulness, the better the results over the long run.[13]

Evidence shows that meditation positively impacts episodic memory, part of the long-term memory that stores information about episodes we experience in life. It is often driven by patterns of associations between memories, and largely determines whether we can think of new things or get caught up in habitual patterns of thought. To be mentally tough, we must be able to break out of rumination, particularly over negative things, and find novel thought patterns to move forward. Meditation can help us become aware of those habitual patterns, and help us break out of those that no longer serve to focus on more productive thoughts and actions.[14]

A review of over 200 studies showed that mindfulness meditation is effective at reducing stress, anxiety, and depression in otherwise healthy individuals, and significantly reduces the rates of relapse in those with major depression. It was also shown to help reduce pain, fatigue, and stress in people with chronic pain. Additionally, it has been suggested that it may also boost the immune system and help people recover more quickly from the cold or flu.[15]

Tell Me How

Mindfulness

Mindfulness activities are often short, simple activities that can be done almost anytime, anywhere. It is the act of really being present. If you are just getting started however, consider making it a priority by scheduling your mindfulness activity for the same time every day. You can start with as little as three minutes and gradually work your way up to longer exercises. No special equipment necessary! Consider trying one of the following practices:

1. Three-Minute Breathing

Sit in a quiet spot and close your eyes. Breathe in and out normally. For the first minute, ask yourself, "How am I doing right now?" Allow the answers to enter your mind without judging them. For the second minute, become aware of your breath. Allow any thoughts that pop up to simply show up and then fade away. During the third minute, expand your attention from your breath to how it feels traveling through the rest of your body. Open your eyes. You're done!

2. Four-Minute Mindfulness Eating

Sit down at a table with something to eat or drink in front of you. Before eating, take one to two minutes to really pay attention to the food and utensils in front of you. Notice color, texture, size, shape, and smell. Then, take a bite or a sip. Notice the taste – is it sweet, salty, salty, spicy, bitter, or a combination of more than one flavor? What is the texture like? How is the temperature? Focusing on what you are eating to the exclusion of everything else helps ground you in the present.

3. Five Senses Mindfulness Activity

This activity helps you to be aware of your environment using all your senses. Take note of the following:

- Five things you can see
- Four things you can feel
- Three things you can hear
- Two things you can smell
- One thing you can taste

Meditation

Meditation requires a comfortable place to sit or lie down and ideally a quiet environment, though the more you practice, the better able you will be to meditate wherever you are. Start small, and work your way up to longer sessions.[16]

1. Guided Meditation

Guided meditations are available online, both for free and through paid subscriptions. They involve listening to a meditation teacher guide you through a meditation of anywhere from one minute to 30 minutes or longer. You can choose a guided meditation that addresses a particular topic, such as decreasing anxiety, or just a general one.

2. Meditation to improve concentration

Set a timer for anywhere between 2-4 minutes. Choose an object to focus on. You may either hold the object or simply observe it. Once you are done observing, start the timer and close your eyes. Think of the object and try to recall every detail. Think of the shape, size, and color. Consider texture, any interesting markings or small defects. When the timer is done, compare your memory of the object with the actual object. Over time, it will become easier for you to accurately recall objects in more detail, improving your concentration overall.

3. Five-Minute Gratitude Meditation

Part of being mentally tough is having a positive outlook on life. It can sometimes be hard to keep that outlook during difficult times, but the practice of gratitude helps shift your attention from the negative to the positive. Find a comfortable place to sit, and close your eyes. Take slow, calm breaths, and allow your body to relax. Then, think of five to seven things in your life for which you are grateful. They can be as small as being grateful that your dog waits for you to come home from work each day with a wagging tail or as big as being grateful for the home in which you live.

You can list them at first but then think about each individually. Focus on how each item on your list makes you feel, perhaps recalling specific scenarios. Finish by taking five slow, deep breaths before opening your eyes.

Many people try mindfulness or meditation activities once or twice. When they find it a bit boring, or difficult, or don't see results immediately, they give up before they really give it a chance. Like any exercise, mental exercise takes time to see results. Use the habit-building techniques from <u>Chapter 7</u> to help make it a part of your daily routine. Much like physical exercise, the days when we least feel like practicing are often the days we need it most. Focus on consistency rather than motivation and reap the benefits of mindfulness meditation.

Action Steps

1. 15-20 Minute Meditation. Once you have mastered the art of the short, under-five-minute meditation practices in this chapter, consider increasing your meditation time by aiming for 15 to 20 minutes daily.

2. Body Scan. A body scan is when you mentally scan your body from head to toe, identifying areas where you feel strong and where you may have pain, weakness, or discomfort. Consider a guided body scan from a free online source the first time, so you can complete the body scan without worrying about "getting it right."

3. Take a class. Classes such as group meditation, yoga, or tai chi are wonderful ways to reduce stress, attend to the body-mind connection, and connect to others. They are wonderful for both beginners looking to build a practice as well as for individuals with years of experience.

Chapter takeaways

- Many successful entrepreneurs and business

people use mindfulness and meditation practices as key foundations for success.

- Mindfulness is the practice of being aware of our thoughts, emotions, and the environment around us in an open and non-judgmental way. It contributes to reduced stress, increased emotional regulation, and improved focus.
- Meditation is the practice of using a technique to train the mind to focus and achieve a state of mental clarity, emotional calmness and stability.
- Four types of meditation are most commonly researched: Focused Attention, Open Awareness/Monitoring,Loving Kindness/Compassion, and Mantra/Transcendental.
- There are two main mindfulness meditation interventions, Mindfulness-Based Stress Reduction (MBSR) and Mindfulness-Based Cognitive Therapy (MBCT).
- A review of over 200 studies showed that mindfulness meditation is effective at reducing stress, anxiety, and depression in otherwise healthy individuals, and significantly reduces the rates of relapse in those with major depression.

9

EMBRACING LIFE'S TRIALS

LEARNING TO ACCEPT HARDSHIPS, OBSTACLES, AND CHALLENGES AS KEYS TO A TOUGHER AND BETTER YOU

"Adversity, and perseverance and all these things can shape you. They can give you a value and a self-esteem that is priceless." — Scott Hamilton[1]

Everyone faces adversity in life, without exception. Adversity is the hardships, obstacles, and challenges we face that significantly impact our well-being. It differs from the small, everyday nuisances that are more inconvenient than anything else. Rather, it is life's challenges that have the potential to leave a lifelong imprint. It is impossible to avoid adversity, so it is important to learn strategies for overcoming it so you can use your weaknesses to make you stronger.

Six Common Categories of Adversity

Adversity shows up in many different areas of life, but most fall under one or more of six general categories, Physical, Mental, Emotional, Social, Spiritual, or Financial.[2] Let's look at each in more detail.

Physical Adversity: The most obvious area of physical adversity comes in the form of physical disability. Many aspects of daily living and the physical environment are poorly designed for universal accessibility. Wheelchair users frequently encounter barriers to public spaces, transportation, and even accessible housing. However, physical adversity need not mean permanent disability. It can show up as an injury, such as a broken arm. It can also present as chronic pain or other forms of illness that affect the functioning of the physical body.

Mental Adversity: Mental illness or mental disorders can make dealing with life's challenges more difficult. Individuals dealing with concerns such as traumatic experiences, addiction, eating disorders, or anxiety disorders to name a few, often feel as though they are fighting their own minds.

Emotional Adversity: Individuals who struggle to regulate their emotions may often feel overwhelmed and out of control. As we learned in Chapter 6, developing our emotional quotient, managing our stress, and getting control over our negative emotions help to build mental toughness so we can be better equipped to face life's challenges.

Social Adversity: Humans are social creatures, even the most introverted among us. Social isolation, difficulty communicating with others, or being on the receiving end of bullying can have a negative impact on our physical, mental, and emotional well-being.

Spiritual Adversity: Spiritual adversity may be most obviously related to religion, but it isn't exclusive to it. From a religious standpoint, spiritual adversity relates to a crisis of faith or a loss of belief in God. From a non-religious perspective, spiritual adversity can relate to a loss of faith in the universe or a belief that existence has no meaning. In both cases, a sense of emptiness may be a common factor.

Financial Adversity: Financial adversity at its most basic is the inability to afford the necessities of life, and can be correlated to extreme poverty. However, financial hardship can also be episodic. Many people suffer temporary financial distress following the loss of a job, extended periods of unemployment, unexpected large expenses following natural disasters or accidents, illness, or other unforeseen challenges.[3]

Sources of Adversity

While most types of adversity fall under the above six categories, they don't occur in a bubble. As a society, we enjoy watching films and reading books about characters who endure extreme forms of adversity under unusual or even impossible circumstances. In real life, most sources of adversity are remarkably mundane, despite the incredible impact they can have on our lives.

The first common source of adversity tends to originate within our immediate and extended families, and with close family friends. Family difficulties remain a massive source of adversity for many people throughout their lives. Divorce, abuse, family arguments, or even the death of a family member are adverse episodes that don't discriminate. All people, regardless of age, sex, faith, social or economic standing are vulnerable.

Social relationships in the form of friendships, romantic relationships, or even acquaintances also have the potential for arguments, misunderstandings, and betrayals. Schooling is a major source of adversity for many people. Whether it's achieving good grades in primary or secondary school or being able to access higher education. Employment is another source of adversity for many adults at some point in their lives. Difficulties finding or keeping employment, relationships with management, colleagues, and clients, or general office politics affect most employees at some point during their careers.

Finally, almost everyone experiences one or more general life changes such as puberty, aging, accidents or illness, disability, experiencing natural disasters, or other unexpected life events that test our mental toughness and ability to bounce back. While we cannot always control their existence, we can try to control how we respond to them. Mentally tough people don't just give in to adversity. They fight back.

Is adversity always a bad thing?

Adversity is most often associated with negative outcomes for mental health and well-being. People who face high levels of severe adversity over a long period tend to have lower life satisfaction and are more at risk for mental health concerns later in life than those who have not experienced adversity or who have experienced moderate levels of adversity. When children grow up in abusive homes, extreme poverty, or spend years living as refugees for example, they are at higher risk of continuing to suffer even once they are no longer living in the same circumstances. Even when individuals mitigate the effects of these events in the short term, it does not necessarily mean that they are building future resilience to adversity over the long term. High levels of sustained adversity can overwhelm individuals and impede their ability to gain skills like stress management and mental toughness.[4]

However, adversity doesn't have to break you down. In fact, while extreme prolonged adversity is linked with detrimental long-term effects, interestingly so does having very low levels of adversity. While extreme adversity can overwhelm our ability to cope, having little adversity robs us of the chance to build the skills necessary to cope with it. Moderate adversity throughout one's life does the opposite. It is associated with better emotional regulation skills over time as there are more chances to practice their development.[5] Moderate levels of adversity actually help us to find our inner strength.[6]

Adversity can be seen as an opportunity to learn and grow. We learn who we truly are and what we are made of when confronted with struggle. We develop mental toughness when we develop effective coping strategies to overcome future obstacles. Additionally, adversity helps provide us with a sense of identity and purpose and can bring into focus the values that are most important to us.

Strategies for overcoming adversity

It might sound counterintuitive, but one of the best ways to overcome adversity is to prepare for it in advance. How? Start by working on building your resilience, emotional regulation, and psychological resistance. Research shows that almost everyone will be exposed to at least one adverse event that has the potential to be characterized as "psychological trauma".[7]

<u>Resilience</u>

As discussed in <u>Chapter 4</u>, resilience is the ability to face adversity and adapt to life's challenges. Resilient people focus on building connections with others, taking care of their mental and physical well-being, and focusing on finding meaning in their lives. When adversity strikes, they have a greater ability to adapt and bounce back.

Building resilience is so important that programs have been designed to help professions that constantly expose their employees to risk, such as rescue workers or the armed forces, to focus on prevention factors to help weaken the effects of stress and avoid the development of mental disorders. The United States Army signed up over 900,000 soldiers and veterans to the Comprehensive Soldier Fitness Program, aimed at preventing or reducing the psychological effects of combat.[8] The program has now been expanded to family members as well, as it has been recognized that it is not only the soldiers preparing for combat who must build resilience.

Building strong connections with others so that you have a network to rely on when you need support is one of the best ways to prepare for the challenge of facing adverse events in the future. But it's also perfectly fine to seek out those connections in the aftermath of a traumatic event. Sometimes even the closest friends and family cannot understand what you are going through, and you need to seek out those who do. A survivor of abuse may need the support of other abuse survivors to heal from the trauma. What's important is to reevaluate your needs often and then act upon them. For more resources and suggestions on building resilience, revisit Chapter 4 as needed.

Emotional Regulation and Psychological Resilience

Increasing emotional regulation improves psychological resistance to life's challenges. Emotional regulation is the ability to adjust your internal state to deal with external pressures and formulate an appropriate response to mitigate their negative impact. Higher levels of emotional regulation are associated with better higher-order executive functioning skills such as problem-solving. Cross-sectional studies have shown that problem-solving skills, planning, and the ability to adapt perspectives are all positively related to the growth of psychological resilience.[9]

Psychological resilience helps people find positive ways to adapt to the negative repercussions of stressors and promotes a pattern of healthy habits following an adverse event. Psychological resilience is when an individual uses both their internal resources and resources in their environment to positively adapt to adversity. Emotional regulation and psychological resilience are connected through the regulation of positive emotions and memories, social support systems, mindfulness practices, and moderate childhood adversity among others.[10]

<u>Overcoming Fear</u>

The above strategies are not meant to suggest it is easy to handle adversity. The instinct to avoid adversity is a normal reaction, borne out of self-preservation. Some adversity is better avoided, particularly when it threatens your health and well-being. When it can't be avoided, some adverse events require the help of a professional to overcome. Abuse, addiction, or extremely dangerous situations should not be taken lightly.

However, in all cases, it takes courage to face life's challenges head-on. Courage is a skill, like any other, that can be developed over time. Confronting difficult situations can be scary, but we can practice getting used to discomfort by putting ourselves into uncomfortable situations willingly. Trying new things, facing a small conflict, or dealing with a difficult person are all ways to flex our mental toughness muscles of courage, grit, and responsibility.

Mental toughness comes from being in control of our emotions, not running from them. We cannot go around our fear. We must go through it to come out the other side stronger. Accepting our emotions, including fear, without judgment allows us to create a practical, effective plan for building mental toughness that allows us to successfully handle the challenges life throws at us.

Action Items

1. Courage! Prepare for real adversity by practicing the skills it takes in a less important environment. Practice putting yourself into situations that require problem-solving, conflict resolution, or other skills that will help build your ability to face your fears, increase your emotional regulation and improve your psychological resilience. If you are someone who avoids conflict at all costs, think small.

Consider returning an item to the store that you bought but never used or negotiating a better rate on your credit card. If these seem easy, then dig deeper. Have that uncomfortable conversation with someone close to you that you've been avoiding for months, for example. Make it personal and a bit scary but not so overwhelming that you push it off even more.

2. *Deal with the past.* Do you still harbor anger, sadness, or resentment from an adverse event you experienced in the past? It's time to come up with a strategy to deal with it and let it go. If you cannot do this alone, consider reaching out to a therapist or other professional for help.

3. *Deal with the present.* What adversity are you currently facing that you can't seem to work through? Try this three-step process to begin the process of growing past it and strengthening your resilience.

Step #1: Let go of your past expectations. Something in your life has changed in a way you don't like or didn't expect, and holding on to the vision you had of your life could be holding you back. Call on your mindfulness practice and break negative thinking patterns to help you accept what is.

Step #2: Take responsibility for what you can and change your mindset. You may not be responsible for the adverse event, but you are responsible for how you deal with it. Change your mindset and decide how you want to move forward in your new reality.

Step #3: Take action. Now that you have taken the time to accept what is and have decided what you want the future to look like in light of your new normal, it's time to put in place the mental toughness to actually make it happen.

We all feel like victims of circumstance sometimes, especially when faced with life events that are extremely difficult to handle and may cause significant trauma. Some adversity cannot be overcome alone, and we need to seek the help of a professional to help us through it successfully. Most of the time we experience adversity occasionally in ways that are hard to handle but not impossible. By focusing on adapting to the circumstances and shifting our mindset to accept our new reality and create a new path forward in light of those new circumstances, we can build resilience and mental toughness and find meaning in difficult times.

Key Takeaways

- Adversity comes in many forms but typically falls under one of the following six forms: Physical, Mental, Emotional, Social, Spiritual, or Financial.
- Sources of adversity tend to come from the types of relationships and situations we all face. Family problems, relationship difficulties, health struggles, and aging are common sources of adversity that almost everyone can relate to regardless of age, sex, ethnicity, or social standing.
- Adversity is unavoidable, but provides opportunities for personal growth, building resilience, and increasing mental toughness by

working on emotional regulation, psychological resilience, and overcoming our fears.

- Rather than running from adversity or our emotions, we must learn to embrace them and use them as a springboard to cultivate positive growth.

AFTERWORD

When you first opened this book, you were challenged to envision your life a year later. Take another moment to do so. What's changed? Are you putting into action the skills and habits you learned in this book and watching your dreams begin to come true? Or are you exactly where you were at the start, doing the same things and getting the same results?

If you made it this far, have read every chapter carefully and worked through the action items at the end of each chapter, I hope your answers to the questions above are filled with excitement and positivity and that you are committed to achieving your strong, specific goals that are designed to align with your values and priorities.

Building mental toughness doesn't end when you close this book. It's a lifestyle, not a standalone skill. Building mental toughness is a lifelong commitment to yourself and the life you want to build. To do so, you must commit to a growth mindset and challenge your limiting beliefs about yourself. Just like the success stories woven throughout the book, I hope you continue to ask yourself, why not me?

Self-awareness will allow you to leverage your strengths and mitigate your weaknesses, develop persistence, resilience, and grit, and increase your self-confidence. Mental toughness isn't reserved for a select few; it is there for the taking by anyone willing to put in the work and see it through.

So, what's next?

It's time to take what you've learned and apply it to setting and pursuing goals that will transform your life, whether in your work, relationships, or any other area you choose to prioritize. Cultivate the types of habits that work for you, rather than against you, and harness the power that mindfulness and meditation can offer to improve your resilience and help manage your emotions.

This book should be your companion as you continue to advance on the path to mental toughness and to building the life of your dreams. Consider working through the action items again if you need a refresher or expanding them to better suit where you find yourself along the journey.

"Don't wait until everything is just right. It will never be perfect. There will always be challenges,

obstacles, and less than perfect conditions. So what? Get started now. With each step you take, you will grow stronger and stronger, more and more skilled, more and more self-confident, and more and more successful." -- Mark Victor Hansen [1]

10 MENTORS OF MENTAL TOUGHNESS

SUPERCHARGE YOUR MIND AND AMPLIFY YOUR INNER STRENGTH WITH 10 STORIES OF MENTAL TOUGHNESS

NOTE TO READER

This book contains information and anecdotes related to real people, from historical icons and political figures to renowned celebrities in their respective fields, both living and dead. These accounts are based on previous interviews, books, public statements, and other platforms available to the public. While every effort has been made to present accurate and reliable data, the author of this book and their associates cannot guarantee the absolute truthfulness of these accounts.

None of the people mentioned in this book, whether dead or alive, have actively endorsed or sponsored this publication. The inclusion of their names or stories should not be interpreted as an endorsement or affiliation with the author, publisher, or the content of this book.

1

THAT PSYCHOLOGICAL EDGE

WHAT IS MENTAL TOUGHNESS AND HOW DID IT PROPEL EACH MENTOR TO GREATNESS?

Michael Jordan. Asha Philip. David Goggins. David Blaine. Oprah Winfrey. Serena Williams. Vince Lombardi. Sara Blakely. Nelson Mandela. Malala Yousafzai.

These ten people come from different backgrounds and represent different worldviews, experiences, and industries. Among them are athletes, entrepreneurs, celebrities, politicians, and advocates. Their approaches to life are different, and yet, they share one common trait: Mental Toughness.

Each of these individuals exudes mental toughness, demonstrating the determination and grit necessary to overcome some of life's toughest obstacles. Abuse, poverty, horrific injuries, imprisonment, and even an assassination attempt. Despite the various challenges they faced, they persisted to overcome them and return stronger than before, reaching even higher levels of achievement and becoming trailblazers in their own right.

Extraordinary people are not born that way. They are built through years of hard work, dedication, and commitment. They strengthen their minds to withstand the criticism, doubt, and hardships that stand in the way of their goals. And they do it by strengthening their minds and living according to the principles of mental toughness.

And so can you.

What is mental toughness?

Mental toughness is an approach to living that embodies the elements of hard work, dedication, perseverance, resilience, and grit. It is applicable to all areas of life and enables individuals to cope with difficult situations, challenges, and stressors in a resilient and positive manner. Mental toughness is not something you're born with, it's something anyone can learn. It isn't one specific personality trait but rather a mindset that encompasses elements of grit, determination, resilience, and other traits that can be developed over time.[1]

Imagine a life where setbacks aren't roadblocks but rather stepping stones toward greatness. Picture a mindset that thrives in the face of adversity, transforming obstacles into opportunities. This is the essence of mental toughness. It is a quality that allows individuals to push past traditional boundaries and accomplish incredible feats.

Whether you are facing difficulties at work, training for a triathlon, or facing pushback in your advocacy efforts, mental toughness will help you overcome those challenges and turn them into stepping stones to success.

Mental toughness is an essential skill in every industry

<u>Sports</u>

Mental toughness is indispensable in the world of sports. Some would argue that the term was first used in that context to describe the incredible psychological strength shown by elite athletes.

For good reason.

The psychological element of sport is a greater determinant of success than physical, tactical, or technical ones, contributing to over 50% of the reason for one's success over an opponent. In wrestling, it is assumed to account for over 80%.[2]

Mental toughness is that "psychological edge" that allows a particular athlete to cope with the challenges of their chosen sport just that much better than their opponent. Athletes with high levels of mental toughness are typically more determined, focused, confident, and in control of their emotions than athletes who are not. They also tend to have higher levels of discipline and competitiveness.[2]

It isn't just the ability to draw on that mental strength during competition that gives certain athletes the edge over others, but the way that it shows up in their training outside of competition. Digging deep mentally can be the difference between training or not when you don't feel like it, or when there's something else more fun to do. It's showing up earlier than everyone else and staying late when trying to get to the next level on a particular skill.

The preparation that goes into being ready is far less glamorous than the excitement of showing up on competition day when the world is watching. Training day in and day out can be exhausting both physically and mentally. It can be lonely, frustrating, and repetitive. Many days the motivation is not there, and athletes rely on their resilience, perseverance, and dedication to keep going and give it their all. The mind helps the body keep pushing even when it wants to quit. That is the role of mental toughness in sports.

<u>Advocacy</u>

Those who spend some or all of their time as advocates also need to develop mental toughness—they need to have the resilience to continue to fight for change despite numerous setbacks and rejections. Resilience refers to the ability to "bounce back" from adversity, coming out the other end even stronger.

When someone finds their purpose in life, resilience is often developed as a way to be able to continue on the path of their dreams, regardless of the obstacles they face along the way. For many advocates, the work they do puts their lives in danger, or they witness the lives of others who are sometimes living in very difficult, heartbreaking realities. They must learn to be adaptable to any situation, making connections, prioritizing their mental and physical health, and managing their stress.[3]

<u>Business</u>

Why do some people thrive in the workplace? Why are some able to adapt their skills to changing demands, and some aren't? Have you noticed that it isn't always the "smartest" or most qualified who move up in a company more quickly than others?

What's their secret?

They are likely to have a growth mindset, a key component of mental toughness. A growth mindset is the belief that a person's true potential is unknown, and that where you are right now is nothing but a starting point for continued self-improvement. Individuals with a growth mindset focus on self-improvement and take responsibility for their actions, rather than blame others for their own shortcomings.[4]

Those with a growth mindset are more likely to succeed in their careers.[5] This is illustrated more clearly in career construction theory, which demonstrates how an employee's readiness and willingness to deal with various job-related tasks and challenges affects their likelihood of developing the adaptability needed to be successful in their chosen career. Those who believe in their ability to continue learning on the job do a better job at rising to the challenges they face at work.

That's because a growth mindset is all about prioritizing hard work and a willingness to learn over innate talent or intelligence. As a result, those with growth mindsets take control of their careers, setting goals for themselves, believing in their ability to learn on the job, and maintaining a positive attitude throughout.

<u>Art</u>

The arts encompass the world of creativity, be it through literature, visual or graphic arts, music composition, the performing arts, or any other medium. For many people, participating in an art form is a hobby or pastime, but for others, it is their passion and the way they make a living.

Except making a living in the arts isn't always easy. Mental toughness in the arts relates to an artist's ability to endure criticism, rejection, and creative challenges while maintaining a strong sense of self-belief and artistic vision. It involves pushing boundaries, embracing vulnerability, and persevering through the highs and lows of the creative process.

Artists often work for months or years on creative pursuits, only to face multiple rejections along the way. They must find the confidence in their vision and abilities to continue moving forward as an artist, without allowing criticism from outside forces to change who they are as artists, taking away their originality and authenticity.

Mental toughness in everyday life

You may not be reaching for the stars as an artist, or hoping to be CEO someday, but that doesn't mean that cultivating mental toughness isn't worthwhile. In fact, it should be considered an essential step to help improve all areas of life. Research has identified multiple benefits of a mental toughness mentality for the average person. Mentally tough individuals are identified with being more likely to be sociable, calm, and relaxed, with lower levels of stress and anxiety. It is also associated with lower levels of depression and higher levels of life satisfaction.[6]

In addition, mental toughness is thought to positively influence how people respond to stress, pressure, opportunities, and challenges. It corresponds to an enhanced ability to cope with failure, with a resilience that allows people to bounce back from failure and use it to work toward future success. It can help you move through life with greater confidence and an attitude that rejects the arbitrary limits of a fixed mindset that would have you believe your abilities are set in stone.

The inspirational power of role models

Role models provide us with inspiration and examples of what is possible. All 10 mentors in this book are regular people who stepped up and accomplished extraordinary things, whether because they set out to be the best in their respective fields, or because they were thrust into the spotlight unexpectedly.

By learning about their journeys and the obstacles they overcame, we can take those lessons that resonate and apply them to our own lives. You don't need to be an elite athlete, media mogul, or social justice activist to learn from and be inspired by their stories. You just need to have the right mindset.

Action Steps

To get the most out of this book, each chapter will have a series of action steps for you to take before moving to the next chapter. Cultivating mental toughness means not just learning about it, but taking action to develop it and practicing the skills over time.

1. Step Outside Your Comfort Zone. If you are serious about developing your mental toughness, getting comfortable with being uncomfortable is key! Over the next week, do one activity a day that is outside of your comfort zone. Don't make it complicated. Consider things like going to dinner alone, wearing something you love but haven't had the courage to wear out, or even asking someone for their number. After completing the activity, write a short note indicating how you felt before, during, and after completing the activity, and whether it's something you would feel more comfortable trying a second time.

2. Celebrate The Small Wins. Every time you complete one of the comfort zone tasks above, celebrate your success! The important thing isn't about how well the activity went, but the fact that you set a goal, faced the fear, and followed through. That is worth celebrating!

Ready to be inspired?

It's easy to see sports figures or celebrities as larger than life. The truth is, they are regular people like you and me, with an extraordinary ability to push through adversity and turn life's challenges into something positive. In Chapter 2, we'll dive into the world of sport and the incredible achievements of one of the best athletes ever, Michael Jordan.

Chapter Summary

- Mental toughness is a psychological attribute that enables individuals to cope with difficult situations, challenges, and stressors in a resilient manner.
- Mental toughness can be applied to any area of life, including sports, advocacy, business, or art.
- Mentally tough individuals are better equipped to navigate and overcome challenges, are resilient, adaptable, and thrive in the face of adversity.
- Mentally tough individuals have a growth mindset, encouraging them to see challenges as opportunities for growth and innovation.
- By studying the journeys of role models from diverse backgrounds, we are exposed to different

perspectives, ideas, and approaches that broaden
our understanding of the world, gaining valuable
lessons that can be applied to our own lives.

2

MICHAEL JORDAN

CAN YOU BE LIKE MIKE? - HOW MICHAEL JORDAN WENT FROM FROM CUT TO CLUTCH AND CARVED A CULTURAL EMPIRE BEYOND THE COURT

One of the greatest all-round players in the history of the game, Michael Jordan achieved levels of success on and off the court that most players only dream about. Under his leadership, the Chicago Bulls won six National Basketball Association (NBA) championships between 1991 and 1998. Jordan is a five-time NBA Most Valuable Player (MVP), six-time finals MVP, 14-time All-Star, three-time All-Star MVP, one-time Defensive Player of the Year, and ten-time NBA scoring leader. Not to mention a two-time Olympic gold medalist.[1,2] He retired a legend of the game, and his name continues to be synonymous with greatness.

Michael Jordan retired from professional basketball in 2003, yet he remains a household name more than 20 years later. Teens who were yet to be born when he played his last game can be seen sporting his jersey and signature Air Jordan shoes. His name and accomplishments are legendary, and for good reason. His work ethic, dedication, and mental toughness inspired generations of athletes who hope to reach even a fraction of the success he enjoyed.

Michael Jordan is widely regarded as one of the greatest basketball players ever. His unwavering competitiveness exemplified his mental toughness, ability to rise to the occasion in pressure-filled moments, and resilience in the face of setbacks and failures. He practiced his own brand of mindfulness and meditation, putting him in the right headspace to dominate on the court.

His life, both on the court and off, is characterized by his unwavering work ethic and confidence in his ability to achieve whatever he put his mind to. The lessons from his life can help anyone gain more success on their own. While it's thrilling to talk about all his success, the real lessons are found in how he handles failures and setbacks. A person's real character, level of resilience, and mental toughness are revealed in the hard times, not the easy ones.

Early failure

One of the most famous stories about Michael Jordan is his failure to make his high school varsity basketball team in his sophomore year. In later interviews, his high school coach spoke out about why he was relegated to Junior Varsity that year. Despite his best efforts, Jordan was described as merely a good shooter and mediocre at defense. He was sent to Junior Varsity to practice those two skills more than for any other reason.[3]

Despite a long and illustrious career, Michael Jordan continues to refer to that first major setback as one of the most significant of his basketball career. It helped turn him into the player he would become, in part thanks to his mother's advice, which was to go to the gym and work harder over the summer to make the team the next year. [3]

Many students would have quit, embarrassed to be dropped to Junior varsity, or convinced that it was a sign that they weren't good enough to keep going. It took maturity, commitment, and a positive mindset to believe in his own ability to improve his level of play enough to move up the following year. Through that setback and subsequent success, he gained the confidence to believe in his ability to continue to improve and find success on the court.

Jordan played two years of college basketball at North Carolina before being drafted to the NBA by the Chicago Bulls as their third overall pick in 1984. He made an incredible start to his professional career in his rookie year, averaging almost 23 points per game, third best in the league.

Jordan won the Rookie of the Year title that first year playing in the NBA. Unfortunately, he then sat out most of his second season with a foot injury. Not letting that deter him, he spent that time recovering and training for his comeback, determined to return stronger than before. He returned to play season three, and proved the critics who felt he had peaked after his first season by leading the league in scoring not only that season, but for the next seven consecutive seasons.[1]

Mental preparation and focus

Part of what made Michael Jordan such a fierce competitor was how he mentally prepared himself for games to have a laser focus on the court. While his particular rituals are specific to his needs as a professional athlete, anyone can learn from his example and benefit from putting their own rituals in place to mentally prepare for their personal life challenges.

In fact, studies show that in sports, ritualized behaviors that athletes believe bring them luck tend to work similarly to the placebo effect, meaning that just believing that a ritual will improve their performance tends to increase the probability of success.[4]

Pre-game rituals

Every athlete has their own set of actions or rituals that they participate in pre-competition, and Michael Jordan was no exception. While some parts of his routine on game day changed over the years, such as switching from being driven to the arena in his early career to driving himself for more alone time later, much of it stayed the same.

According to reports, he would typically take a nap and have a meal of steak and potatoes before heading to the arena. Rather than listening to aggressive music, he preferred the calm, soothing sounds of Anita Baker. Dressed to the nines, he arrived in style, always in a suit that gave off power vibes.

He insisted on being taped up for the game last and often didn't touch a basketball until 20 minutes before the game. He believed that he could make playing the game easy by practicing hard. Famously, he wore his University of North Carolina basketball shorts underneath his NBA shorts for each game to remind him of where he came from. Additionally, he wore a new pair of Air Jordan sneakers for each game, tying the laces himself. He then performed a specific series of warm-up exercises and shooting routines before the game started.[5]

These rituals may sound odd to an outsider, but they were one of the keys to his success. By practicing mindfulness in how he completed every single item (and then some!) before the game, those rituals helped him focus his mind, establish a sense of routine, and enter a state of optimal focus and readiness.

Mental rehearsal or visualization

The practice of mental rehearsal, better known as visualization, is now such a core practice for athletes that they often hire coaches specifically to help them master this aspect of their performance. In the late 80s and early

90s, it wasn't quite as popular, and yet Michael Jordan used it to his advantage.

He would often run through what he wanted to happen in his mind, not just in words. Visualization is the actual act of seeing the actions in your mind as though you are doing them. More than that, it's feeling them as though they are real. He would imagine himself making successful shots, executing flawless moves, and achieving success game after game. The calm focus, the confidence, and the precision execution of every move took place in his mind long before it ever did on the court.

As a result, he got to a place in the game where he was present in the moment. By visualizing his performance beforehand, he was able to become fully immersed in what was happening right then and there, rather than worrying about the next play or the outcome of the game.

Players often get ahead of themselves, thinking about hypotheticals rather than focusing on what is happening in that second. Michael Jordan could seemingly block out distractions, including the crowd's noise and the players' trash-talking on the opposing team, to completely focus on the task at hand, making split-second decisions that often led to game-changing plays.

He was known for his belief that 80% of the game is mental and only 20% is physical, so he put a lot of faith in the mental preparation to be ready, resilient, and mentally tough.[6]

Devastating personal loss

Almost a decade after his rookie season, Michael Jordan faced a devastating personal setback in the untimely death of his father. James Jordan Sr. had been driving home from a funeral in the early hours of the morning on July 23, 1993, when he pulled over to the side of the highway to get some rest. He fell asleep in his vehicle, a red Lexus that had been a gift from Michael.

Two teenagers saw the car at the side of the road sometime later, and decided to steal it. The plan was to tie up James Sr. and leave him at the side of the road while they left in the vehicle. They claim that he awoke during the robbery, and that the teen with a gun panicked and shot him, killing him on the spot.

They changed plans and decided to dump the body in a vat at a waste treatment plant, but when they discovered it was closed, they dumped it in a South Carolina swamp instead. According to reports, the teens did not know who they had murdered until they later checked his wallet. The teens were convicted of his murder after his body was found.[7]

The loss was devastating for Michael Jordan. Initial reports erroneously speculated that his father's murder could be related to Michael's gambling debts, insinuating that he may have had an indirect link to the murder. He was grieving the murder of his father, while also dealing with the added scrutiny and judgment those reports generated. He became more aware of the dangers of being so famous, realizing that anyone could be following him or targeting him at any time.

His father had been one of his biggest supporters, attending almost all of his college and NBA basketball games and encouraging his development as a player from a young age. Michael Jordan referred to his father as having been his rock, and his loss left him struggling with immense grief. He had just won his third NBA championship a little over a month prior to his father's murder, and had been considering retiring from the sport. His grief following his father's murder led him to follow through, retiring from the sport at the height of his career.[8]

Perseverance and comebacks

Jordan's father had been a big baseball fan, and believed that his son could be one of the few athletes to successfully pursue a professional career in more than one sport. Jordan had never really considered the possibility seriously until after his father's death.

He joined the Chicago White Sox's minor league team in Alabama, determined to make it to the majors. Some speculated that the move was an attempt to fulfill a lost dream of his father's, while others believed that he was using baseball as a distraction from his grief. But those who played baseball with him describe a hardworking athlete with great respect for the sport.

Jordan went from the best in the world at basketball, to essentially a trainee in the minor leagues. By all accounts, he showed up tirelessly and was open to learning. The skills and body awareness needed for baseball are vastly different from basketball, so he needed to learn to control his body in completely different ways. He knew that he was setting himself up for criticism and potential ridicule, but chased his goals anyway.

He quit the sport not long after in 1995. Some say it was because he failed, but others point to the strike by the Major League Baseball (MLB) players' union. Jordan refused to cross the picket lines to be a replacement player if the strike was not over by the time the season began. Still, others report that he had been itching to return to basketball, privately practicing at the Bulls' training facility.[9]

Michael Jordan's growth mindset allowed him to believe that he could excel at anything he put his mind to and that he was not relegated to just basketball. Part of his ability to make this change resulted from his perseverance. Many people fear failure, but Michael Jordan firmly believes that failure is a necessary part of the process on the road to success. His ability to learn from failure, persevere through hardship, and come back time and again set him apart from the crowd.

He returned to the NBA for the 1995-1996 season.[1] He returned a changed player, more encouraging of his teammates and more inspired by the love of the game. Despite concerns about his ability to recapture his dominance at the time of his first retirement, he led the Bulls to the best NBA season record at the time, 72-10. He led the Bulls to three consecutive NBA championships and won MVP each season before retiring again in 1998.

He later returned to the league a final time, playing two seasons with the Washington Wizards and retiring for good following the 2002-2003 season.[1]

Legacy

Michael Jordan was not what anyone would call an easy teammate. Not even him. As the leader of the Chicago Bulls, Jordan's demanding nature often made him a tough teammate. However, he focused on being the best player he could be and pressured his teammates to do the same to create a championship team.

And it worked.

Jordan inspired and motivated others to work harder and aim higher. He was willing to lead by example and focused on the teamwork that was needed to create a culture of winning in the organization. He worked hard and expected everyone around him to be as committed as he was to improving daily.

Even now, more than twenty years after his retirement, his legacy resonates with athletes and others worldwide. His mental toughness, competitiveness, and relentless pursuit of greatness continue to serve as a blueprint for success and inspiration and may continue to do so for future generations.

Action Steps

1. Create a Ritual. Where would creating a ritual be of use to you in your life? Perhaps you run the Monday morning meeting but find it so stressful that you have difficulty sleeping Sunday night. Identify one area where a ritual would help you be more comfortable or more successful, and then create a 2-5 step ritual that can reliably be done beforehand. Make the steps easy to remember and simple to complete and put them into practice immediately.

These rituals should be distinct from your everyday routine, but not become a distraction. For example, perhaps you have a pair of lucky socks you wear for big meetings, and a special coffee mug or water bottle that you keep at hand to provide a sense of comfort and familiarity. Arriving in the meeting room 15 minutes early to go over the agenda can also be a simple ritual that helps improve your confidence.

2. Visualization. Using the same scenario as in step one, visualize yourself completing each step of the activity from before you start until right when you finish. The more details, the better. Play each step like a movie in your head and try to imagine what it will feel like as you move through each step.

3. Bounce Back From Failure. Setbacks and failure are a part of life, so rather than running from them, learn to embrace them to learn from your mistakes. Every failure carries valuable lessons that can make you better the next time if only you take the time to learn them. Think about a recent setback or failure you experienced. Find just one thing you can work on right now to help improve your chances of success in the future.

Michael Jordan's legacy is as strong today as it was immediately following his retirement. Despite the large number of great players who followed, his name continues to be kept in the conversation when discussing the greatest of all time. From one athlete to another, Chapter 2 dives into the life of Asha Philip, in a story of setbacks and success that feels like it was taken straight from the movies.

Chapter Summary

- Michael Jordan had a number of pre-game rituals he practiced, helping him focus his mind, establish a sense of routine and familiarity, and enter a state of optimal readiness.
- He used the technique of mental rehearsal, or visualization, to build confidence, enhance focus, and develop a strong belief in his abilities by visualizing his desired outcomes.
- His ability to be fully present in the moment allowed him to make split-second decisions on the court.

- He is known for his perseverance through difficult times and comebacks.
- Following a short retirement to play minor league baseball, his return to professional basketball was met with doubts, but he went on to win three consecutive NBA championships from 1996 to 1998.
- His legacy on and off the court continues to resonate today. His demanding nature, focus on teamwork, willingness to lead by example, and relentless pursuit of greatness serve as a blueprint for success and inspiration.

3

ASHA PHILIP

CAN YOU SPRINT PAST THE IMPOSSIBLE? - HOW
ASHA PHILIP CONQUERED BROKEN BONES AND
SET BLAZING RECORDS THROUGH GRIT AND
THE PURSUIT OF EXCELLENCE

With pressure to focus on excellence in a single sport, not many young athletes put their energy into competing in two distinct sports, yet this is what Asha Philip did. As a young athlete, she competed in both trampoline, a gymnastic sport, and track, an athletic one. She achieved success in both.

She won gold in the 100m sprint at the 2007 World Youth Championships and was also a World Junior Mini Trampoline Champion, successfully competing in both sports simultaneously. At the age of 16, she was world champion in both. She seemed poised for greatness as she moved up to the senior levels in each sport.[1]

Until a life-changing injury threatened her future as an athlete.

During the 2007 Trampoline World Championships in Quebec, Canada, she suffered a horrific injury. Her

180

trampoline performance was phenomenal, hitting all the right moves. As she jumped into her dismount however, something went wrong. She landed on both feet, but her right knee buckled beneath her, appearing to "disappear." The injury dislocated her knee, tearing every ligament, and fracturing a bone. Most people thought her athletic career was over, in any sport.[2]

She was advised by many to give up on her dream of competing in sports again and focus instead on simply regaining the proper function of her right knee. She rejected that advice and instead, using her mother's belief in her ability to make a full comeback as fuel, she dug deep into her well of mental toughness and committed to a full recovery and comeback.[3]

In fact, it would take her three years of grueling rehabilitation and training to be able to run properly again. Her first success was simply being able to get back on her feet with the help of crutches. From there, she had to go back to basics: learning to walk. Progression wasn't linear. As she healed from her knee injury, other minor injuries followed, making rehabilitation that much more difficult.[3]

Despite experiencing multiple injuries and setbacks during the recovery process, Asha Philip persevered. She had missed her chance at qualifying for two Olympic games due to injury, and was determined to qualify for the games in Rio de Janeiro in 2016.

She made her return to athletics in sprinting full-time in 2014. From there, she qualified for Team Great Britain and made her Olympic debut in 2016, where she helped her team win bronze in the 4x100 meter relay at the age of 25. She went on to win a gold medal in the 60-meter sprint at the 2017 European Indoor Championships and another 4x100-meter relay bronze at the 2020 Olympic Games in Tokyo.[4]

Her commitment to training and rehabilitation was driven by her mental toughness and resilient approach to training and recovery.

Overcoming injury: Challenges, resilience, and determination

It's hard to believe that Asha Philip was so young, just 17 years old, when she suffered such a devastating and life-changing injury. The level of maturity she showed when faced with a multi-year rehabilitation calendar is remarkable.

She was faced with the prospect of never being able to walk or run properly again. She went from the top of her sport to losing everything in a split second. She did not allow the frustration and disappointment of being written off as a "has-been" to change her mind about mounting a comeback. And she refused to be overwhelmed by the uncertainty around her future abilities. The circumstances would have been intimidating for an adult to handle, yet she was still a teenager.

So, how did she do it?

She relied on her mental toughness and surrounded herself with others who believed in her and wanted to see her succeed in the face of adversity.

Facing challenges

Starting over from such a devastating injury required commitment and consistency. One of the main tenets of mental toughness is discipline and persistence over motivation. Let me explain.

Motivation is fickle. It can help you get started on something, providing that initial hit of adrenaline when the idea of something first takes hold. However, motivation isn't always a faithful friend. Have you ever just not felt like doing something? Lack of motivation, that feeling of not wanting to, is often why people give up before they really get going.

Instead, discipline is a much better predictor of success. When you have discipline, motivation is nice but not essential. Discipline means that you show up because you have committed to doing so and you show up consistently every time.

Persistence is the ability to continue along a course of action, even when faced with difficulties or obstacles along the way. Attributes include grit, resilience, resolve, and determination. Asha consistently worked toward her goals, even when progress was gradual and felt slow. Her persistence paid off over time.

Mental toughness and work ethic

Mental toughness is often confused with only being about resilience, which is incorrect. Resilience is certainly a huge part of mental toughness, but it isn't everything. That's not to say Asha wasn't resilient. But it wasn't just resilience that turned her into a two-time Olympic medal winner. Her work ethic and positive attitude played key roles.

Asha Philip returned to the world of elite sport through a combination of different approaches and strategies:

<u>Work ethic:</u> A constant dedication to rehabilitation and sport, putting in countless hours of practice, conditioning, and skill development. Asha's work ethic meant that she showed up consistently, did all that was asked of her and more, and pushed herself to her limits, always striving to improve. Keeping a positive attitude and her eye on the ultimate prize helped her to make it through the darkest times.

<u>Resilience:</u> This is the ability to not give up in the face of adversity. It is sometimes characterized by one's ability to "bounce back" from each setback or failure. While that sounds easy, it's incredibly difficult to continue trying again in the face of difficult obstacles and failures. Asha's decision to return to elite sports and dedicate several years of her life to achieving that goal is the epitome of resilience.

Mental Toughness: Believing in herself and her ability to thrive under the most difficult circumstances, cultivating the perseverance, dedication, and resilience to achieve her goals. She successfully employed the 4 Cs of mental toughness:

1. *Control:* She controlled what could be controlled, including her own emotions and reactions to her circumstances.
2. *Commitment:* She committed herself to her rehabilitation and long-term goals, working through temporary lags in motivation.
3. *Challenge:* Despite the seeming unfairness of such an injury at a young age, she looked at her rehabilitation as a challenge to overcome rather than a tragedy to endure.
4. *Confidence:* Asha summoned the confidence needed to believe that she could overcome her injury and achieve her goals.[5]

Flexibility: Rather than stubbornly staying on the same path, she was able to pivot to what would work best under the circumstances. For Asha, that meant leaving the world of competitive trampolining behind to focus solely on running.

Confidence: She remained confident in her abilities, even when outsiders doubted her, by developing the skills needed to be successful.

Physical Training: A combination of strength, speed, and agility training, along with cardiovascular conditioning. She needed to learn to walk, then to run, and then to be able to run with the confidence and speed needed to compete against other elite athletes at the highest levels of competition.

Growth Mindset: Choosing to believe that her abilities could develop and grow rather than feeling limited by her current circumstances. Those with a growth mindset believe that their mental and physical potential is flexible and can change with effort and time. Individuals with a growth mindset focus on self-improvement, take responsibility for their actions, and look for solutions to problems rather than blame others for their own shortcomings.[6]

Support: She surrounded herself with people who believed in her and motivated her with their dedication and positivity. This included coaches, trainers, and other support staff who guided her training program and provided her with the necessary resources and expertise to rehabilitate from her injuries and improve over time.[7]

Lasting inspiration

Asha Philip has inspired young and old athletes for over 15 years. One of few athletes to dominate in two distinct sports and hold world championship titles in the same year, she occupied a very privileged space in elite sport prior to her injury in 2007. As a young, Black woman from Britain, she was also an inspiration for many young athletes from underrepresented communities in the UK and worldwide.

However, perhaps even more inspirational than her early accomplishments is how she returned after such a devastating injury to become a two-time Olympic medalist, narrowing her competitive focus to dedicate her training to sprinting. Her patience and dedication during the nearly four years following her injury showed maturity beyond her years, an amount of self-confidence few people possess, and a level of mental toughness that we should all aspire to develop.

Asha Philip's pursuit of excellence and drive to improve constantly can inspire individuals striving for greatness in their respective fields, not just athletics. Her unwavering commitment to self-improvement can motivate everyday individuals to push their limits and set high standards for themselves, no matter how long it takes to achieve their goals.

Action Steps

1. Replace Limiting Beliefs. We all have stories we tell ourselves about our personal abilities or lack thereof. What limiting belief have you been telling yourself to avoid trying something out of fear that you won't succeed? Try this exercise: Write down one thing you want to accomplish but have been avoiding. On one side of the paper, write down all the limiting beliefs you have been telling yourself that are holding you back. On the other side, replace those beliefs with a positive thought that will encourage you to take action instead.

2. *Pivot.* This might sound counterintuitive but hear me out. Being mentally strong doesn't mean pushing through everything, regardless of the outcome. It also means knowing when you have had enough or when another thing might work better. Grit versus Quit! Asha Philip switched focus from trampolining to sprinting and found great success in her new sport. If you have been continuing along a specific path that is no longer working for you out of fear of failure, maybe it's time to pivot to something else. For Asha Philip, quitting sports wasn't the answer, but switching sports was. How can you pivot to achieve greater success?

3. *Find Your Team.* Some people like to brag about being lone wolves and achieving all their success alone, but the truth is that the most successful people admit they didn't do it alone. Asha Philip relied on family, trainers, coaches, and the support of other athletes to help her return to sport and reach the top of her game once again. Surrounding yourself with others who want the best for you will help you achieve greater heights than going it alone. Is there an area in life where you would like to see greater progress? Consider finding a mentor, a coach, or a group of people in person or online who are reaching for

a similar goal to connect with and watch your progress accelerate.

Asha Philips defied the odds following a devastating injury to become an Olympic medalist and continues to train to reach new heights. She credits her mental toughness as one of the key elements of her success, surrounding herself with people who believed in her potential.

From sprinter to endurance sports, Chapter 3 goes into the life and mindset of David Goggins, a man who went from a self-professed individual with limiting beliefs to a highly accomplished endurance athlete by pushing his own boundaries in his pursuit of personal growth.

Chapter Summary

- A world champion in trampolining, Asha Philip injured her legs during a world championship competition in Quebec, requiring extensive physical rehabilitation.
- Her commitment to training and rehabilitation was part of her immense work ethic—putting in countless hours of practice, conditioning, and skill development, including strength training, speed drills, agility exercises, and cardiovascular workouts.
- She sought out positive, encouraging people with a growth mindset who supported and motivated her on her journey.

- Asha Philip's pursuit of excellence and drive to improve herself constantly is a source of inspiration for anyone striving for greatness. Her story can motivate others to push their limits and set high standards for themselves in any field.

4

DAVID GOGGINS

A CALLOUSED MIND AND AN UNSHAKEABLE WILL - HOW TO CLIMB OUT OF HELL AND ONTO THE ULTRAMARATHON TRACK OF YOUR BEST SELF WITH DAVID GOGGINS

David Goggins is not the type of guy who worries about hurting your feelings. He isn't known for mincing his words, making excuses, or cutting anyone any slack. His brand of mental toughness is the kind that demands everything you have, and then asks you to dig deeper for more.

Because whatever it is he sees someone else give, he makes sure to give that much more.

David Goggins is a former Navy SEAL and ultra-endurance athlete who has overcome numerous physical and mental challenges, including childhood abuse, obesity, and a heart defect, to become one of the world's toughest athletes. He practiced consistency and applied several mental toughness techniques to overcome his adversity, and he believes that anyone else can do it, too.

David had a difficult childhood. His father was a widely loved figure in town, but at home he was a completely

191

different person, beating his wife and kids over the smallest things. His father controlled the finances, the decisions, and ensured that David's mother was completely reliant upon him. While the family was not short of money, Goggins, his mother, and his brother were short of safety and security.

Before the age of ten, David was spending his evenings in the rink, sanitizing shoes and sleeping on a sofa in the back office until the early hours of the morning. He struggled to stay awake at school as a result, often sleeping through key lessons.

When his mother finally found a way to leave, she, David, and his brother ended up in a small town in the Midwest, just 15 minutes from where the Ku Klux Klan held public demonstrations as late as the 1990s. David was one of the only black kids in school, and his lack of a solid educational base came back to haunt him. Over time he learned to cheat, and developed a self-described "thug" persona, pretending not to care in order to hide his true feelings of inadequacy.[1]

It wasn't until he was a teenager and wanted to follow in his grandfather's footsteps in the Air Force that he developed his first mental toughness technique for self-improvement: The Accountability Mirror.

The Accountability Mirror

David Goggins took a good look at himself in the mirror

as a teenager and admitted a hard truth—he was his biggest enemy.

Did he have a hard childhood? Yes.

Was he behind at school as a result? Yes.

Was his mother struggling as a single mother? Yes.

Were these obstacles good enough reasons to give up and declare that it was too hard to succeed at his dream of joining the Air Force?

Absolutely not.

He realized at that moment that his life was his responsibility, and success or failure was in his own hands. To succeed, he had to show up and be accountable to the only person who mattered: himself. He had to look at himself in the mirror every day and take accountability for what he had accomplished that day, as well as for what he had not.[1]

The Accountability Mirror habit may have started in his teenage years, but he used it through to adulthood. He turned his life around so completely that he became the only man to complete Special Forces training in all branches of the U. S. Military.[2]

<u>How it works</u>

1. Take a good look at your reflection and call yourself out. Goggins started his days looking in the mirror and taking stock of where he was in his personal development, particularly the areas for improvement. His personal approach is direct, blunt, and brutally honest. He doesn't advocate couching failures in indirect language, but instead prefers to be his own harshest critic, identifying his weaknesses before anyone else can point them out.

By being honest and direct, you can get to the improvement phase more quickly than spending months making excuses or feeling sorry for yourself.

He called himself out on his failures and encouraged himself to do better. He identified the areas he wanted to improve and set goals that reflected the high standard he set for himself. He would think about the day before, and if there was something he was unhappy about, he wrote it on a post-it, stuck it to the mirror, and then went about fixing it. As a high school student, many of his failures had to do with trying too hard to fit in with his peers and being lazy at home and at school.

2. *Focus on the small, immediate things to improve your life, and work your way up to bigger goals.* David started by working on his appearance and his daily chores. He chose an aesthetic, shaved head and face, and committed to it daily. He also committed to completing all his chores to the best of his ability without being asked.

His reasoning for this was simple: If he couldn't even manage to commit to personal grooming and daily responsibilities, how could he expect to scale up to accomplishing his biggest long-term goals?

He started small and committed to continuous improvement.

3. Post your goals in the mirror, keeping them small and achievable. Goggins believes that seeing your goals this way is more effective than having them typed up in an app. He used good old-fashioned Post-it notes, where he wrote down each goal and then stuck them to the mirror. Whenever he reached a goal, he removed a Post-it and replaced it with another.

The key is keeping the goals small and achievable so you can experience success and forward movement quickly. For example, if you want to lose 50 pounds, you might start by putting up a Post-it with a goal of losing just two pounds. When you reach that, you remove it and add another with two or five more pounds, until you reach your goal. This is similar to the chunking method of goal achievement, where a big goal is broken down into smaller, bite-sized chunks.

4. Repeat, daily. David Goggins believes that only you can keep yourself accountable to yourself. Seeking outside validation means that your internal sense of self is dependent on the opinions of others. You are responsible for your own life, your own successes, and your own failures. Blaming your life's circumstances or the hardships you face for giving up or failing to put in 100% is not an option. He believes that most people never bother to find out what they are really capable of.

Overcoming obstacles: Physical transformation

Mental toughness is a journey, not a destination, and like most journeys, there will be setbacks along the way. Goggins realized his dream of being accepted for Air Force training, but came up against an obstacle he was not able to mentally overcome at the time, that of open-water swimming. He could swim, but not in the way that was required for the possibility of parachuting into the open ocean to perform a rescue operation.

As his swimming difficulties became more obvious as the training progressed, he struggled with how to improve. During a routine medical check, it was discovered that he had sickle cell trait. He was given the choice to continue his training or to quit the training program. He used the diagnosis as an excuse to end his training, and it was a decision that haunted him for years after. While he had a legitimate reason to not continue, he knew in his heart that it was fear that caused him to take that out when presented with it.

In the years that followed, his disappointment turned to depression and self-loathing, and his previously disciplined routine fell apart. He gained over 100 pounds in a short period, took a job as an exterminator in the evenings, and ate his feelings in the form of late-night donut runs and huge breakfasts at his mother's house.

The beauty of mental toughness, however, is that it is something that can be cultivated at any point in one's life. Failure is a part of life, but learning from failures can turn hard times into strength. Goggins found his chance to cultivate his mental toughness again and overcome his fears when he saw an ad recruiting for the Navy SEALS, the elite primary special operations forces in the United States.

David Goggins decided that he was going to become a Navy SEAL, despite his earlier aversion to swimming. The problem was, he was almost 300 pounds and needed to get down to 190 pounds to qualify for training in the space of less than three months. In addition, he needed to teach himself the material to pass a difficult written exam. [1]

He decided to get comfortable with discomfort and embarked on an extremely difficult diet, exercise, and study routine to prepare for acceptance into the training program. Goggins believes that when cultivating mental toughness, you are, in fact, callusing your mind.

Callusing the mind

Much like your hands develop calluses to protect them from the ongoing friction borne of physical labor, Goggins believes that when we push through perceived limitations and overcome the desire to quit or give in to a "victim mentality," we are callusing our minds.

This is why he advocates for doing your best work when you are the least motivated, and for continuing to push forward when your intrusive thoughts tell you to stop. Goggins took that mindset to the extreme—running marathons while injured—but you don't have to go to those lengths to benefit from the technique.

Callusing the mind can mean refusing to listen to those who tell you something can't be done, or that your goals are unrealistic. It can mean running another mile when you really want to stop and walk. It can also mean refusing to allow failure to define you. David often takes this to the extreme, pushing himself to accomplish feats few others have even attempted.

He has completed Navy SEAL training and became only the 36th African American Navy SEAL in history, held the world record for the highest number of pull-ups in 24 hours, and has completed over 60 marathons, ultramarathons, and triathlons. And he couldn't have accomplished any of it without callusing his mind against failure.[1] It may sound as though David Goggins is a superhuman, strangely incapable of failing, but he is open about his failures and how he uses them to come back stronger.

Goggins had to endure Navy SEAL Hell Week training three times before successfully completing it. Hell Week is considered the most difficult training in the U. S. Military, consisting of 5 ½ days of full physical training on less than four hours of sleep a night. It tests physical endurance, strength, pain and cold tolerance, the ability to perform under pressure, and yes, mental toughness. It is as much a test of mental strength as it is of physical endurance. So tough, that only around 25% of trainees successfully complete the week.[3]

He attempted the pull-up world record unsuccessfully twice before achieving it on his third try. And he ran his first 100-mile race woefully unprepared, and is open and honest about the various training and execution mistakes he has made in other ultra-endurance competitions.[1]

Failure isn't the problem. It's the inability to take the lessons that failure offers to improve the next time around. When you callus your mind to failure being a setback and look at it as a stepping stone instead, what you can accomplish is limitless.

Kaizen method for self-improvement

Running ultramarathons and breaking world records don't happen overnight. Goggins himself is an advocate of breaking down big goals into smaller, consistent, ongoing improvements. To break the pull-up world record he calculated that he would need to complete six pull-ups per minute, and focused his efforts on improving his ability to complete those six for longer and longer periods. As the cliche says, A journey of a thousand miles begins with a single step.

Goggins uses a methodoloy that has been compared to the kaizen method to build up to incredible accomplishments, and then to keep on going. Commonly known as the 1% improvement technique, rather than aiming for a fixed improvement goal, the idea is to continuously improve in small increments over time.

Kaizen is a philosophy made famous by Japanese businesses looking to improve performance incrementally over time. In fact, kaizen is one of the core values of global automotive giant Toyota, integrating it into their production system.[4]

When applied to personal development, the goal is long-term development over short-term gains that often also end up being short-lived. Often, people set audacious goals and get off to a flying start, only to find that when that initial motivation peters out, so does their progress, and eventually they leave the goal behind.

Or they push through, reach a big goal, and then find themselves floundering for what to do next. If the goal is to participate in a triathlon, once you've reached that goal, then what? Many people complete one triathlon and then never compete again. Some stop training at all and lose their previous fitness levels.

The kaizen method is almost the antithesis of those approaches. Rather than aiming for a goal that has a beginning and an end, the kaizen method focuses on small, incremental improvement in any area of life. In this way, self-improvement becomes a lifelong goal, as the goalposts keep moving.

Kaizen requires you to take the long view. Outside of a business setting, the idea of improving by increments can be applied to any task, physical or mental. If you want to read 30 minutes a day, you might start by reading for five minutes first, gradually increasing your reading time until you reach your goal.[5]

Does this mean you have to keep increasing your daily reading time to eventually take over your day? Of course not. Once you've met your reading goal you can either add on additional time, or pivot to improve in a related but different way. You might want to branch out into different types of books, or different topics, or different levels of difficulty. The technique helps you reach goals, yes, but the real goal is incremental, ongoing self-improvement.

For this method to be effective, it requires flexible thinking, a new way of approaching goals, and a commitment to continuous improvement. Becoming fit enough to participate in a triathlon and successfully completing one can still be goals, but once they have been accomplished, continuing to work on your fitness levels should still be a priority. What that looks like may shift, however. You may choose to never participate in another triathlon, but the goal of continuous improvement means that you will still be interested in improving your physical fitness, or perhaps setting your sights on a new physical challenge.

David Goggins has since retired from the armed forces, but continues to set new goals for himself that challenge his body and mind. No matter where you are in life, you too can commit to pushing your boundaries and redefining what's possible.

Action Steps

1. Use Personal Obstacles as Fuel and Eliminate Excuses. David Goggins encourages people to start their personal transformation by making a list of the obstacles standing in the way of reaching their goals. They can be personal circumstances like poverty or domestic abuse, or societal ones, like racism or sexism, but they should all go on the list. That list then serves as the fuel for overcoming each one in whatever way you can. Take control of those things within your control and start to find ways around the ones that aren't.

2. Create Your Own Accountability Mirror. In order to really develop mental toughness, you need to be tougher on yourself than anyone else. In other words, you need to be accountable for your actions. Unless you are accountable to yourself first, you will never reach your goals. Goggins uses an accountability mirror. Stick Post-it notes on a mirror with small goals, such as reading for 20 minutes a night every evening this week. When the goal is reached, remove the Post-it and replace it with the next goal. Each time you look in the mirror with those goals posted on it, you need to be accountable for your progress to the only person who matters, yourself.

3. Practice the Kaizen Method. Commitment to small, continuous, incremental improvements in every area of your life. Focus on being 1% better tomorrow than you are today. Rather than setting one big goal that you achieve and then forget about, the kaizen method focuses on long-term achievement due to small, daily improvements.

David Goggins overcame abuse, poverty, and racism to become an elite Navy SEAL, a Guinness World Record holder, and one of the most decorated endurance athletes in the world—and he continues to seek out new and exciting challenges. From one form of endurance to another, Chapter 5 introduces David Blaine and his unique form of endurance activities.

Chapter Summary

- David Goggins overcame childhood abuse, poverty, and racism using mental toughness techniques and a no-excuses plan of action to use adversity as fuel for accomplishing his goals.
- The Accountability Mirror is his way of facing his harshest critic, himself. By chunking goals into smaller milestones via Post-it notes, he keeps track of his progress daily and overcomes limiting beliefs.
- He adopted a mentality that allowed him to push through mental and physical barriers, refusing to give in to self-doubt, complacency, or the victim mentality, voluntarily subjecting himself to challenging situations to push his limits every day.
- He calls the process of building mental toughness "callusing the brain," essentially

enabling him to exercise consistency even when unmotivated, and to work his hardest precisely when he doesn't feel like it.

- Practicing kaizen means that you are constantly improving, in small increments. This approach means that you are never done evolving and changing for the better, so when you reach one goal, it becomes a stepping stone for another.

5

DAVID BLAINE

THRIVE WHEN THE HEAT IS ON - HOW TO TRANSFORM PRESSURE INTO PERFORMANCE FUEL THROUGH THE ALCHEMY OF SUPERNATURAL FOCUS LIKE DAVID BLAINE

Times Square has seen a lot of crazy stunts, but a man suspended in a block of ice in the square for almost three days *on purpose* may take the cake.

And David Blaine can take the credit.

In November 2000, the street magician turned endurance artist embarked on what many people believed to be nothing more than an illusion: He was encased in a block of ice placed in Times Square in New York City to last 72 hours. The ordeal was filmed, and regular passersby could approach the block of ice to view the man inside.

Blaine was really in there, battling freezing temperatures and suffering from sleep deprivation. He fell short of his 72-hour goal but made it for 63 hours, 42 minutes, and 15 seconds before being cut out with a chainsaw. He was later taken to the hospital out of fear that his body would go into shock, and he later said that it took an entire month to heal.[1]

Impossible? Seems like it should be.

Instead, it was the culmination of months of training to be able to endure the extreme temperatures, sleep deprivation, boredom, confinement, and being on display that were all part of the deal.

While Blaine may guard some of the secrets of his street magic, he is quite open about what goes into his endurance stunts. He started training at home alone for this particular event, soaking in an ice-filled bathtub and moving to stand-up dunks in bigger tanks for extended periods.

Enduring the cold wasn't the only skill he needed to develop. Since he would be standing the entire time, with only two inches of space between him and the ice, he needed to learn to stand still for hours, even napping in that position.

Then, the more technical aspects. He fasted for five days beforehand and used a catheter for his urine. He did not eat solid food during the feat but had water and oxygen delivered via tube. He wore special boots to help encourage blood circulation to avoid developing blood clots. His exposed skin was covered in a warmth-sealing gel worn by ocean swimmers to prevent hypothermia, and doctors monitored his body temperature. The entire scenario wasn't magic; it was science.[2]

It was only one of several incredible endurance events he would embark on for the world to see, such as being buried alive for a week or spending 44 days without food in a transparent box suspended over the River Thames.

His ability to push his mind and body to the limit and endure extreme physical pain and psychological challenges demonstrate his mental toughness. He achieved all his feats through mindfulness, meditation, and consistency.

Physical strength, mental endurance, and psychological resilience

Physical strength

David Blaine's fascination with endurance started as a child. He talks in interviews about being born with legs that were turned inward and having asthma as a child, which meant that he could never compete with other kids in activities that required speed. However, he learned that if he could hold out long enough, he could often beat those same kids at activities that called for endurance, like long-distance swimming or running.[3] The real-life version of *it's not a sprint; it's a marathon.*

He used that fascination with endurance to push himself to do more and more difficult endurance challenges that defy what we think should be possible. One such feat was breaking the world record for holding his breath underwater in 2008, which he did on national TV during a broadcast of

The Oprah Winfrey Show. David Blaine submerged himself in a sphere of water and held his breath for 17 minutes and 4.4 seconds, a world record that was later confirmed.[4]

How? He still uses these techniques, incorporating physical and mental training to move toward his goals incrementally, not just jumping in all at once. He starts with small goals, building up to bigger ones over time. In one interview, David Blaine explained that he didn't start by saying he would hold his breath for almost 20 minutes. Instead, he started trying to train himself to hold it for 5 minutes and then moved up from there.[3]

This applies to all the endurance stunts he performs. Once he moves to a level where professional help is required, he works with the appropriate professionals to overcome the next hurdle. This could mean a physical trainer, a doctor, a coach, or any other professional who can provide him with the right guidance and expertise.

Training his body to stay still in one position for days, as he did in the ice block, in a coffin, and even standing on a pillar, takes a massive physical effort. Training his body to survive only on small amounts of water for days at a time or to withstand extreme temperatures and even physical pain requires considerable time, effort, and mental toughness.

However, the mental work needed to complete feats of endurance on David Blaine's level is equally demanding.

<u>Mental endurance and psychological resilience</u>

Sometimes, we let our minds put limits on ourselves that have little to do with our physical abilities. When thinking about any of David Blaine's endurance challenges, the idea of trying what he did is scary. He is not immune to that fear himself and uses a type of exposure therapy to help him mentally prepare to put his body and mind through such extreme stress.

Exposure therapy

Exposure therapy was developed to help people confront their fears in a controlled, safe manner. When something is worrisome, scary, or a cause for anxiety, avoidance is the go-to response of many people. Unfortunately, we can't always avoid things in life. Using exposure therapy helps him face those fears by simulating stressful environments. Adding progressive exposure forces the brain to face those stressors repeatedly, building up progress over time.

Different variations of exposure therapy exist and are helpful in various types of circumstances.

- In Vivo Exposure: This involves directly facing a fear in real life. A person who fears dogs may be taken to a dog park, introduced to a therapy dog, and eventually encouraged to pet or walk a dog.
- Imaginal Exposure: Rather than physically facing a fear, a person may be asked to talk about, write about, or otherwise imagine an object, situation, or activity to break free of the fear.

- Virtual Reality Exposure: Technology can simulate scenarios that cause us fear and anxiety, such as taking a virtual roller coaster ride.
- Interoceptive Exposure: Interoception involves physical sensations. This type of exposure can be about simulating the physical feelings of what you fear. Rapid heart rate, hot or cold, or other physical sensations can be recreated away from the triggering stimuli to allow a person to develop strategies to deal with them.[5]

Mastery of mind control

Many people think that physical endurance activities are about how much the body can handle, but that is only part of the equation. The mind truly needs to be mastered, for the mind is the master of the body. Many athletes talk about the importance of being in the zone, using visualization techniques, or generally keeping a positive attitude during challenging times to keep going. David Blaine excels at the mind game.

<u>Meditation and mindfulness</u>

Meditation has the power to transform the brain literally. Studies show that people who meditate regularly actually experience physical changes to the brain for the better. Just eight weeks of mindfulness meditation showed an increase in the brain in areas that control learning, memory, emotions, and self-referential processing, in other words, the area that makes you think too much about yourself. Mindfulness training helps individuals shift the focus of their thinking from themselves to the present moment. This can be helpful in regulating emotions.[6]

The same eight weeks led to a decrease in cell volume in the amygdala, the area of the brain that processes fear, anxiety, and stress, and led to study participants reporting better mood overall.[7] Meditation and mindfulness help David Blaine to cultivate calm thoughts, a centered state of mind, and control over his thoughts, emotions, and reactions.

Visualization

Similar to Michael Jordan and Asha Philips, David Blaine visualizes his success before it happens in real life. Rehearsing his performances in vivid detail over and over again ahead of time makes the actual performance easier to pull off because he doesn't have to think about each detail as it happens.

Studies show that visualization actually allows a person to enter an altered state of consciousness. Functional MRIs show that brain waves change during visualization, enhancing performance, self-confidence, and even healing properties.[8]

Visualization is about more than just "seeing" success. When done correctly, it engages all five senses, but inside your mind. Imagine yourself preparing to give a speech in front of a room of people. Visualization doesn't begin with the act of the speech but much earlier. Imagine your outfit, the size of the room, and how the podium will feel under your hands. Consider your walk to the front, the lights above, and the feel of the water you sip before you start.

The more detail you can visualize, the better. It may mean visiting the location in advance if you can or looking at photos or videos of it to get a better idea for your visualization.

Visualization does not substitute for actual physical preparation, but it can be extremely helpful in preparing the mind. David Blaine can't exactly stand on a 100-foot pillar for 35 hours in preparation for standing on a 100-foot pillar for 35 hours as the actual stunt! Physical training and frequent visualization practice were needed to prepare both body and mind.

<u>Breath control</u>

Learning to control your breath is about more than just deep breathing to calm you down in stressful situations. Breath control is essential for achieving mental focus and regulating physiological responses. Through deep breathing exercises, David Blaine can control his heart rate, calm his nerves, and maintain a steady state of mind. Adapting to rapidly changing circumstances requires mental agility and responsiveness in high-pressure situations.

Controlled breathing has been common in Eastern cultures for centuries and is integral to many ancient practices, such as yoga and meditation. In Western cultures, it has taken longer to be adopted as a critical part of daily living, but more scientific studies confirm the benefits. Controlled breathing techniques positively impact autonomic, cerebral, and psychological flexibility. It also reduces stress and anxiety.[9] Stress management is key to managing emotions and cultivating a positive mindset to boost resilience and mental toughness.

Lessons on mental toughness from David Blaine's performances

Blaine thrives on pushing the limits of both his physical and mental abilities. He moved from classic magic and illusions to feats of stamina and endurance that test the boundaries of what is possible. Still, we don't have to strive to stand in blocks of ice or hold our breath underwater for long periods to be able to learn from his preparation for these acts and integrate some of these lessons into our own lives.

1. <u>Growth and Achievement:</u> To grow as individuals and achieve things beyond our imagination, we must be willing to step outside our comfort zones and embrace the challenges that come with that. We need to listen to our wants and needs and push past those who tell us we can't succeed. Sometimes, we are the ones telling ourselves that our goals are unreachable. By doing something uncomfortable daily, no matter how small, we begin to realize that many of the limits we think we have are self-imposed and not real at all.

2. <u>Mind-Body Connection:</u> Beyond the physical acts themselves lies the incredible amount of invisible mental work that went into preparing for them. We must strengthen our minds as much as, if not more than, our bodies at times. Willpower, commitment, attitude, resilience, mental toughness—these get David Blaine through when his physical body is ready to give up. When faced with pain, exhaustion, or doubt, we can tap into our mental reserves of grit and determination to push through temporary discomfort.

3. <u>Be Fully Present:</u> Many of David Blaine's endurance stunts are performed live in front of an audience, and distractions are inevitable. By fully engaging in what he is doing, ignoring the distractions as much as possible, and channeling all his energy into the task, he enhances his performance and makes the most of each moment.

Action Steps

1. Practice Progressive Exposure. Exposure therapy as a therapeutic exercise for trauma is best left to a professional. Still, if you want to increase your tolerance and endurance for something simply uncomfortable, you can embark on it solo.

Choose something you have been avoiding out of anxiety or mild fear. Choose one or more progressive exposure techniques discussed in the chapter and confront them head-on.

2. Practice Endurance and Willpower in Everyday Activities. In simple terms, practice finishing what you start. Choose an activity that you often need to complete. Think small, like cleaning the kitchen each evening before bed. Use whatever techniques you need to, including modifying how you finish, slowing down, or eliminating non-essential elements, but find a way to finish the activity every time. This builds endurance, willpower, and psychological resilience. Build up to bigger challenges over time.

3. Break Goals into Chunks. David Blaine talks a lot about setting small goals for himself and then restarting them again to build up to much bigger ones over time. You may want to swim ten laps at the community pool but give up after three each time you try. Chunk that goal into ten one-lap goals. After each lap, concentrate on finishing only the next. Repeat until you reach the bigger goal.

David Blaine's life and career are a testament to the physical achievements we are capable of should we put our mind to it. In Chapter 6, we will learn about a woman who defied the odds by becoming an enduring presence in the homes of Americans and individuals worldwide for over 25 years.

Chapter Summary

- To physically prepare for demanding challenges, David Blaine engages in physical training and preparation that includes progressive exposure to push his limits incrementally. Exposure therapy expands his capacity to endure physical discomfort, stress, and fear.

- Incorporating meditation and mindfulness practices into his daily routine helped Blaine to achieve a calm and centered state of mind and control his thoughts, emotions, and reactions.
- Using visualization techniques to rehearse performances mentally in detail and successfully completing each challenge in his mind primed his body for success.
- He uses breath control and deep breathing exercises to achieve mental focus, control his heart rate, calm his nerves, and maintain a steady and stable mind even in high-pressure situations.
- He emphasizes the importance of mental flexibility, adaptability, and quick thinking and trains his mind to be agile and responsive. His approach highlights the importance of the mind-body connection.
- Growth and achievement often require stepping outside our comfort zones, embracing challenges, and being fully present in the moment.

6

OPRAH WINFREY

DO YOU DARE SPEAK YOUR TRUTH? - DISCOVER
HOW OPRAH WINFREY USES THE POWER OF
AUTHENTICITY AND EMPATHY TO BREAK
BARRIERS AND IGNITE CHANGE

"And you get a car! And you get a car!"

Even those who know little about Oprah Winfrey tend to be familiar with the stories of her annual "Favorite Things" episode of her famous talk show, *The Oprah Winfrey Show*. Every year, as preparation for the Christmas holiday season, Oprah would make a list of her favorite things to give for the season. The show typically aired in November, Thanksgiving week.

The gifts ranged from the practical to the indulgent, the affordable to the exorbitantly priced, locally made to imported goods. Oprah selected each item carefully, knowing that her influence and the exposure on her show and in her monthly magazine could launch a small business into the mainstream or turn an unheard-of item into that season's must-have gift item.

What made the annual episode even more special was that it was taped in front of an unsuspecting studio audience of around 300 people, each member of which went home with every single item on the list. Since show episodes were taped sometimes months in advance, audience members weren't aware of the show topic until taping began. In 2004, almost 300 people went home with not only the list of items, but a brand-new car!

Pontiac had sponsored a promotion on the show to give away vehicles worth around $30,000 each to every audience member, resulting in over $8 million worth of vehicles gifted in one of the biggest television giveaways ever.[1]

Oprah's generosity of spirit is one of her lasting legacies, whether through those years of "Favorite Things" giveaways, her involvement in philanthropic endeavors, or her dedication to standing up for what she believes in. Far from being born with the kind of money that would make giving easy, Oprah overcame a difficult childhood of poverty and upheaval to become one of the richest women in the world. Her decision to use large sums of money in the service of others is just one way in which she has given back, now that she can.

Today, Oprah Winfrey is a media mogul. She successfully overcame various setbacks to become one of the world's most influential and successful women. She has helped others by speaking openly about her struggles with abuse and self-doubt and how she used those experiences and a growth mindset to build resilience and empathy.

Early life and challenges: Mental toughness as a survival tactic

Born to a poor, unwed teenage mother in rural Mississippi in the 1950s, she was raised on her grandmother's farm. While few would have predicted her later success in life, she showed her natural intelligence at an early age. Her grandmother taught her to read by age three, and Oprah spent hours reading books and memorizing Bible verses to recite to neighbors and family friends. Ahead of her peers in kindergarten, she was moved up to Grade One with students older than her.[2]

When her grandmother fell ill, Oprah was sent to Milwaukee to live with her mother in a small inner-city apartment. She moved back and forth between her mother's apartment in Milwaukee and her father's home in Nashville. While living with her mother, Oprah endured sexual abuse by a cousin and other men close to her mother, beginning at age nine and lasting several years. She started acting out, eventually falling pregnant at 14 and giving birth to a son who did not survive.

Despite her difficult childhood, Oprah knew she was destined for more. She pushed through the obstacles in her path to excel in school, earning a full scholarship to Tennessee State University. While in college she read the news on a local radio station. A Nashville news anchor heard her and offered her a job in television. At first, she attended college during the day and worked at the news station in the afternoons and evenings, but eventually dropped out of college one credit short after receiving a job offer that would allow her to pursue a career in broadcasting full-time.

Though young and inexperienced, Oprah believed in herself and her ability to achieve anything she put her mind to. She became the first African American news anchor in Nashville at 19. She then followed that up with a move to Chicago to host a morning talk show. That show would later become *The Oprah Winfrey Show.*

Oprah Winfrey has used her success to launch several business and philanthropic endeavors, and her influence has been crucial to casting a spotlight on the issue of sexual abuse.

The Oprah Winfrey Show and public scrutiny

That early decision and belief in herself led to an incredible groundbreaking career on television. Oprah's talk show ran for 25 seasons and became the most watched in television history. Its success helped her to become the world's first Black female billionaire and the world's only Black billionaire for three years running from 2003.

Oprah herself was central to what set *The Oprah Winfrey Show* apart from its competition. In a time when talk shows were often sensationalist, her show focused on the shared human experience from a more compassionate perspective. Rather than having guests on for shock value, she focused on showcasing people and issues that highlighted something about the shared human experience.

Oprah often expressed that while not every audience member would have the same experiences as her guests, her responsibility was to help the audience connect with the guests by understanding them better. In one episode about racism, Oprah helped guests understand what it felt like to be discriminated against for something out of their control. She separated audience members by eye color in a recreation of Jane Elliott's famous eye color experiment. Audience members with blue eyes were treated worse than those with brown eyes.[3]

By addressing difficult and sometimes painful topics thoughtfully and carefully, she ushered in a new generation of daytime talk shows. She made topics that were once considered taboo the subject of dinner table conversation.

Mental toughness and resilience in the face of adversity: Beef with the cattle industry

Oprah is known for her uncompromising standards, willingness to fight for her beliefs, mental toughness, and resilience in the face of adversity. In 1996, she faced one such test, when a segment on her show about food safety led to a lawsuit.

Specifically, it was the part about beef. At the time, "mad cow disease," an illness that affected cattle, had been confirmed to have spread to humans in England via the consumption of beef, resulting in death in several cases. The segment included an explanation of how the problem might eventually be found in American cattle, prompting Oprah to declare that she would no longer be eating hamburgers.

Within two weeks of the show airing, the price of cattle plummeted in the United States, prompting a lawsuit from the cattle industry, blaming Winfrey's segment for the drop. They used a recent law widely known as the "veggie libel law" that had been passed in Texas in 1995, which made it illegal for someone to make false statements about the safety of food.[4] The Texas cattle industry believed that Oprah's statement about never eating a hamburger again was directly responsible for the fall in prices.

For many celebrities, the prospect of a drawn-out court case in a state across the country wouldn't have been considered a good business or even something that was worth the time. A public apology, or clarification, followed by an out-of-court settlement may have made the problem disappear as quickly as it arrived.

Instead, Oprah stood firm. Although it took almost 18 months to actually get to court, she had to move production of her television show from Chicago to Texas for several weeks. Oprah took the case seriously. Testifying on her own behalf, she later explained that for her, the case wasn't about beef at all.

It was about free speech and responsible journalism. And Oprah was willing to defend those beliefs in court, displaying mental toughness, courage, resilience, and the self-belief that she was fighting for something worth fighting for.

The jury voted unanimously in her favor, and speaking outside the courthouse following the verdict, she made that point clear by referring to the case itself as an attempt to "muzzle" her freedom of speech. She reminded those watching that she was descended from people who struggled and died for freedom of speech, so she refused to give up hers.[4]

Overcoming failure with gratitude, service, and presence

Oprah's show was a smashing success, but not everything she touched turned to gold. She suffered several public failures, but considers her 1998 film adaptation of Toni Morrison's novel *Beloved* as her greatest public failure. With Oprah at the helm in the starring role, and big-name actors such as Danny Glover and Thandiwe Newton starring alongside her, the film was expected to be a critical and box-office smash.

Instead, Oprah's agent called her the day after opening night to tell her it was already a flop.[5] Despite a marketing push by Disney and an hour-long special on Oprah's show before its release, the film only took in $21.1 million after four weeks at the box office.[6]

The news sent her into a tailspin, and she refers to the aftermath as the only time she has been depressed in her life. She asked her chef to make macaroni and cheese, and she binged-ate as much as she could.

Once the dust settled, she got to work bouncing back, using three practices.

1. <u>Gratitude</u>: Although she was disappointed that the movie hadn't been a success, she focused on being grateful for what she had, not on what she lacked. She became grateful for the work itself, letting go of the results.

2. <u>Service</u>: Oprah realized that the work of adapting the book into a movie and putting it out into the world was an act of service, by making the content of the book accessible to more people. She felt that the work itself was the important offering to the world. She had been focusing on the box office results and audience reception, which was misguided in her opinion. The work was the service to others. The results were secondary.

3. <u>Presence</u>: She focused inward on her depression for about six weeks before looking outward again and recommitting to being really present in her life and in the lives of others. She used that practice to connect with others, making them feel seen and in return focusing on something other than herself and her own concerns.[7]

Philanthropy, social justice, and empowerment

When everything else falls away, her generosity and philanthropic acts will be her lasting legacy. She established the Oprah Winfrey Foundation in 1987 to empower and support the education of women and children worldwide. She launched the Angel Network in 1997 to fund scholarships, build homes, and help everyday citizens create their own projects. It raised over $80 million before closing in 2010, contributing to 60 schools being built worldwide, along with youth centers, scholarships, women's shelters, and homes.[8]

Her donation to the Smithsonian Museum of $21 million remains the largest single donation to date. And there were many, many more.[8] Oprah's focus is on service, rather than the dollar value, believing that everyone has something to give. Her conviction that she lives her life in service to others has made a positive change in the lives of millions of people worldwide.

She has also stood up for social issues, being instrumental in the passing of the National Child Protection Act in 1993, a bill that required the creation of a national registry of convicted child abusers and mandatory reporting. She testified about her personal experience of childhood abuse, and it is widely believed that it was her influence that helped it pass. It was later dubbed "The Oprah Bill."[9] Whether using her voice, her time, or her money, Oprah has made standing for something and acts of service central to her lifestyle.

Through her Book Club, in which she chose a different book monthly, encouraging her followers to read along with her, Oprah became a champion for literacy and diversity in literature. Her choices highlighted diverse voices, including people of color, LGBTQ+ authors, and others whose voices traditionally have not been amplified in mainstream media.

Her choices highlighted social issues, including race, gender, and sexuality, and have even been credited with helping to change the publishing industry. The success of the books she chose for her book club showed that mainstream America could be enticed to purchase literature from diverse authors offering different worldviews.[10]

Action Steps

1. Stand for Something. In many ways, Oprah is a living example of putting your money where your mouth is. Her philanthropic endeavors run into the millions, supporting issues she is passionate about, including girls' education. She also stood up against child and sexual abuse and fought for free speech. What issue do you stand for? What can you do to make a difference, no matter how small?

2. Practice Gratitude, Service, and Presence. Oprah overcame her greatest failure by reframing the experience. Rather than viewing the box office bomb as a failure because it wasn't commercially successful, she turned to being grateful for the work and the ability to be of service by adapting the novel to be put out into the world and focusing on being present with others rather than dwelling on herself.

- Gratitude: Begin a gratitude practice. Consider writing down 1 thing you are grateful for daily.
- Service: Focus on how you can be of help to others, whether in your job, your community, or even a stranger on the street. Focus on how it feels to focus on the process and not be obsessed with the outcome.
- Presence: How often do you multitask in the presence of others? Check your phone during a conversation? For the next week, focus on being completely present when speaking with others. Show an interest in their lives, and really listen when they speak.

Oprah continues to break barriers in her sixties, shining a light on issues she feels deserve more attention, including those related to aging and ageism, and shows no signs of slowing down. From one powerhouse to another, Chapter 7 moves back to the world of sport and the incredible career of Serena Williams.

Chapter Summary

- A difficult childhood didn't stop Oprah Winfrey from pursuing her dreams as an adult, drawing on her own inner strength to develop the mental toughness needed to succeed in a difficult industry.

- Oprah's authenticity, empathy, and ability to connect with her audience and tackle serious topics changed the daytime talk show landscape, eventually becoming the highest-rated talk show in television history.
- Oprah has been open about her experiences with poverty, abuse, racism, and body-shaming, and how she used those experiences to fuel her personal quest for ongoing self-improvement and spiritual development.
- Her 1990s defamation lawsuit by the cattle industry highlighted the issue of responsible journalism and free speech.
- Mindfulness and gratitude form a core part of her approach to daily living, which she shares with her audience in a multitude of ways.
- Oprah has dedicated much of her life to helping others through her book club, her network OWN, and her philanthropic endeavors.

7

SERENA WILLIAMS

THE BENEFITS OF CAUSING A RACKET - SERENA WILLIAMS' ASCENT TO THE TOP THAT BROKE THE MOLD, TRANSFORMED THE GAME, AND INSPIRED A GENERATION OF STEEL-WILLED DREAMERS

Serena Williams caught the world's attention at the 1999 U.S. Open Grand Slam tournament in New York City when she won her first grand slam at 17 against Martina Hingis, then World Number 1. Serena bounded onto the court in white-beaded braids, a protective hairstyle popular in the African American community, gold jewelry, and a toned, strong physique. Playing in her first Grand Slam Final, she was not expected to win, yet she took the match in straight sets.[1]

She was the first Black woman to win a Grand Slam singles title since 1958.[2] And she was just getting started.

The spectators in New York had no idea that they were witnessing the start of an era for the world's future female tennis player with the most Grand Slam wins of the Open Era, dating back to 1968. Serena spent 186 consecutive weeks at number one in the World Tennis Association (WTA) rankings, a record she shares with

Steffi Graf. She spent 319 total weeks at number one over the course of her career: four Olympic gold medals, 23 Grand Slam singles titles (the most by any tennis player in the Open Era, male or female, at the time of her retirement), 14 Grand Slam Women's Doubles titles won with her sister, Venus—the list goes on.[3]

Serena Williams is arguably the best tennis player of all time. She is known for her fierce competitiveness, resilience, and mental fortitude on the court. Despite numerous setbacks and injuries throughout her career, she continued to compete at the highest level. Through goal setting, persistence, managing her emotions and stress, and developing positive habits, she overcame adversity to rise to the top of the game.

Introduction to tennis: A life-changing event

Legend has it, Serena's father, Richard Williams, watched a women's tennis final in 1979 and realized that the winner of the match won more money than his annual salary. At that moment, he told his wife they needed to have two daughters and raise them to be tennis stars.[4]

Serena Williams was born in Michigan in 1981 but raised in Compton, Los Angeles. Tennis was not a popular sport for young Black females in the lower-income L.A. neighborhood when Serena Williams was a little girl. That didn't deter her father, Richard Williams, from introducing Serena and her older sister, Venus, to the sport when they were young by taking them to the public tennis courts in Los Angeles to practice.

Although he had no background in playing or coaching tennis, Richard Williams felt he saw talent and potential in his girls. Private coaching was not an option at the time due to financial constraints, so he took on coaching Serena and Venus himself. A strict coach, the girls spent long hours practicing under their father's critical eye.

As the Williams sisters' potential became more evident, the family moved to Florida in 1991 so they could train at a tennis academy before moving to the professional circuit in the mid-1990s.[5]

While the initial media assumptions were that Venus would be the bigger star, Serena's father always said that Serena was the stronger of the two. He was never shy about expressing his opinions about his girls, even famously predicting the two would meet in the 1999 U.S. Open final, which Serena eventually won because they were too fast and too strong for the other competitors.[4]

Overcoming challenges and developing a growth mindset

Racism and discrimination on and off the court

Unfortunately, as Serena won more matches, the attention she received wasn't all positive. Tennis is notoriously a sport for the wealthy and white, and she didn't fit the mold.

The first high-profile racist incident of her professional career came just two years following her Grand Slam win in New York at the Indian Wells tournament. Her sister Venus pulled out of her semi-final match due to tendonitis, but rumors flew that it was a set-up to allow Serena to play the final and win the tournament. Rumors fueled resentment, which, in some cases, led to racist slurs being shouted at Serena while on the court and at her father and sister in the stands.

Although Serena won the tournament, she was so traumatized by the experience that she boycotted playing there for the next 13 years. She later spoke about how difficult the experience had been for a young woman of just 19 years.[4]

Sadly, Serena would battle body-shaming and racist and sexist abuse throughout her entire career. Much of the attention has been focused on her body. It didn't match the aesthetic of some of the popular players of the time, like Anna Kournikova or Maria Sharapova—specifically, White, blonde, and thin. Deemed too big, too strong, too muscular, too manly, too fat, Serena has heard it all, often via mainstream media, even once having her body compared to a monster truck.[6]

On many occassions, the comments against Serena were downright racist and sexist attacks. Following her fifth Wimbledon win, a professor at Washington State University compiled a collection of tweets from spectators and tennis fans referring to Serena as a gorilla to highlight the racist treatment she endured as a player and a person.[7]

Other times, the comments stemmed from ignorance or were supposedly lacking malicious intent—yet they were equally troubling and harmful. For instance, fellow tennis professional Caroline Wozniacki imitated her on-court by stuffing towels into her shirt and the back of her skirt to emphasize her chest and buttocks, and multiple reporters referred to her weight being a detriment to her movement or a source of masculine strength the other players lacked.[7]

Serena Williams was not immune to the effects of these ongoing, disgusting attacks. Nonetheless, rather than give them much public attention, she channeled any negativity she received off the court into motivation that she used as fuel to prove her skills on the court, becoming the best in the world. To do that, she needed to develop an unshakeable amount of self-confidence.

Turning negativity into motivation: The role of self-confidence

Self-confidence refers to your trust in your ability to rise to challenges, believing you have the character and skill to succeed. It involves a high degree of self-awareness, including intimate knowledge of your personal set of resources and skills and an awareness of your impact on others.

True self-confidence lies in believing in your own abilities to accomplish your goals, regardless of what anyone thinks. To develop it, you often must "fake it until you make it" first, using any number of techniques to feel stronger and more powerful. One technique often suggested for increasing self-confidence is to dress for success. Taking control of your image can lead to real improvements in self-confidence.

For Serena Williams, part of that was creating her own personal armor on the court with the outfits, hair, and nails she chose for each tournament. Instead of shying away from criticism, she leaned into those physical and aesthetic traits that made her unique and displayed them defiantly while she won tournament after tournament on her way to the top. Her iconic on-court hairstyles over the years earned her a retrospective visual essay in *The New York Times*.[8]

Despite harsh criticism from former players when she started her own clothing line while still competing professionally, Serena's fashion brand proved to be a success, earning her fashion awards that supported her vision of creating a brand of inclusive women's fashion.[9]

Honing her skills also increased Serena's self-confidence on and off the court, helping her realize her own potential and drown out the relentless onslaught of outside opinions. An intimate knowledge of her personal strengths and weaknesses, coupled with her characteristic grit and mental toughness, helped her shut off the outside world in the moments it mattered most.

Mental toughness when it counts the most: Grand Slam finals

Serena showed her ability to come back from deficits in matches time and again, even against players who were ranked higher than her. Her never-give-up attitude, self-confidence, and self-belief empowered her to make the necessary mental and strategic adjustments to turn the tide in her favor when all seemed lost.

One of her most memorable comebacks was in 2007, winning the Australian Open after having missed most of the 2006 season with a knee injury and entering the tournament unseeded, ranking 81 in the world. She went on to win the tournament against one of her biggest rivals of the time, Maria Sharapova.[10]

From her first Grand Slam win to her last match, her resilience and ability to retain her focus under the most intense scrutiny and pressure became her trademark. Her father called her "mean," insisting that it was what helped her win under pressure, but perhaps a better description would be that she had grit.

Psychologist Angela Duckworth defines grit as a combination of passion and perseverance for a singularly important goal and believes it is the hallmark of high achievers in every domain.[11] That perseverance set Serena apart from her competitors many times over.

Grit is believed to be more important than even talent, allowing someone to be more successful than someone with innately more talent by focusing on the following areas:

1. Deliberate efforts to improve one specific area of importance.
2. Focusing on this effort with 100% intensity.
3. Ask for continuous feedback and complete this loop until excellence is achieved.
4. Do it all with passion.[11]

Serena Williams used her grit to power through adversity, embracing the pressure and attention she garnered in those big matches and performing at her peak when it mattered most.

Off-court influence

Serena's visibility and success have had a significant impact in many areas, including diversity representation in sport and brand endorsement, inclusion, and gender equality in sport and society. Her unlikely ride from a young Black tennis player trained by her father in Compton to the greatest of all time has shattered barriers for the next generation. She has inspired countless young boys and girls, particularly those from underrepresented backgrounds, to pursue their dreams and challenge societal norms.

Philanthropic endeavors

Off the court, Serena spends a generous amount of time and energy giving back to others. One such endeavor is extremely personal. In 2003, her oldest half-sister was murdered in a drive-by shooting in Compton in what was a case of mistaken identity. Serena and her family started the Yetunde Price Resource Center in Compton to provide healing and trauma-informed resources to families affected by violence in honor of her sister.[12]

She has also been a United Nations Children's Fund (UNICEF) Goodwill Ambassador since 2011, supporting the UNICEF Schools for Africa initiative to provide affordable education for marginalized and vulnerable children. Serena also supported the #EveryChildAlive campaign that provides affordable, quality healthcare for mothers and newborns. She speaks extensively about her own health crisis following the birth of her daughter.[13]

<u>Enduring legacy</u>

Serena Williams retired from tennis following the U.S. Open in 2022, but her legacy extends beyond her impressive number of Grand Slam titles and Olympic medals. She inspired and continues to inspire new generations of young athletes who don't fit the expected norm to pick up a racket and get on the court.

Serena pushed back against racist and sexist stereotypes and resisted the urge to give in to body-shamers who called her too masculine to be a female athlete. She proved that being feminine and strong, feminine and muscular, and feminine and aggressive were not mutually exclusive.

Since retiring, Serena has continued to win prizes, becoming the first athlete to win the Fashion Icon award from the Council of Fashion Designers of America. Her clothing brand is inclusive, striving to ensure all women have access to great design. Her legacy will soon be cemented further, as she will be inducted into the National Women's Hall of Fame in March 2024, alongside Ruby Bridges and other notable women in America's history.[14]

Action Steps

1. Build Your Self-Confidence. Self-confidence is a key aspect of mental toughness and believing in your own abilities is always more important than what others think of you. By cultivating the image you present to the world, you can help you feel in control and help increase your self-confidence. Serena used her clothing, hairstyles, and even nails to project an image of confidence when she stepped out on the court. How do you want to show up in the world?

2. Mount a Comeback. Is there anything you have given up on that you wish you hadn't? Do you secretly wish you could try again? Consider making it happen. Perhaps you gave up on learning a new skill because life got in the way. Perhaps you loved playing in a band in high school and miss the camaraderie of regular jam sessions. Whatever it is, consider picking it back up again. Allow yourself to do something badly at first while you demonstrate the grit and determination to keep at it until you see the improvement you hope for.

3. Lift Up the Next Generation. Serena is an incredibly talented athlete, but much of what makes her an inspiration to others has little to do with tennis. Her incredible ability to be her authentic self and embrace what makes her different from her competitors captured the hearts and imaginations of people worldwide. What makes you unique that you can share with others to lift them up? How can you give back to the next generation?

From the tennis court to the football field, from athlete to coach, Chapter 8 delves into the world of one of the greatest football coaches in the game's history. This proves that mental toughness is about more than just being able to play the game; it is also essential for leaders to successfully motivate their team to greatness.

Chapter Summary

- Despite financial constraints and no experience with the game, Serena Williams' father recognized her and her sister's talent and potential and took it upon himself to coach them from a young age.
- Serena faced racism and discrimination during her early years as a player and used these experiences to develop resilience and a growth

mindset to keep developing her skills and proving her detractors wrong.

- Her ability to maintain focus under pressure during Grand Slam matches and to turn the tide of matches in her favor in crucial moments is a testament to her mental toughness and never-give-up attitude.
- Her success as an athlete and entrepreneur has impacted diversity, inclusion, and gender equality in tennis and beyond.
- She has spoken out against racial injustices and the systemic barriers faced by athletes of color.

8

VINCE LOMBARDI

TOUGHING IT OUT IN THE TRENCHES - HOW VINCE LOMBARDI STEERED UNDERDOGS TO THE PINNACLE OF GLORY AND FORGED A LEGACY OF CHAMPIONS

"Winning is a habit."[1]

It's the 1967 Super Bowl game. There are 16 seconds left on the clock. The Green Bay Packers are down 17-14. The ball is at the one-yard line, meaning they need to get it over that line to win the game, which would bring the Packers their third National Football League (NFL) championship in a row, a feat no other team has ever achieved since postseason play began in 1933.

The only problem? The temperature is -13 degrees and the field is a sheet of ice.

The safe play is a pass into the end zone. A completed pass secures a win, and an incomplete pass stops the clock long enough to kick a field goal, tying up the game and sending it to overtime. But Vince Lombardi has never been a coach who plays it safe.

Instead, he gambles on a surprise play despite the icy field, despite the high probability of players slipping and being unable to hold off the defense.

The quarterback takes the snap and, instead of throwing or passing the ball off to another player, dives into the end zone for the touchdown and the win. The gamble pays off and the Green Bay Packers win their third straight championship, a record that stands today.[2]

Vince Lombardi was a legendary football coach who led the Green Bay Packers to five NFL championships. Lombardi emphasized the importance of mental toughness, discipline, and teamwork in his coaching philosophy. As a leader, he focused on setting goals and achieving them, he expected his team to perform their best in every game. He didn't believe that winning happened to you on occasion but rather saw it as a daily habit formed in every action in all areas of life.

Unlike many of the other mentors in this book who either started their paths to greatness at a very young age or who continued their paths for decades, Vince Lombardi made his impact on the world of football quickly, and then was gone less than a decade later, dying from an unexpected illness before his time. That his influence remains as strong as ever is a testament to the impact he made on the sport in such a short time.

Simplicity and execution: A winning combination

Vince Lombardi stepped into the head coach position of the Green Bay Packers, almost a virtual unknown. His only professional coaching experience was as an assistant coach for the New York Giants for five seasons, during which the team enjoyed considerable success. Prior to that, his only head coaching experience was as a high school football coach, followed by two assistant coaching jobs, one at a college and the other at West Point Military Academy.[3]

When Lombardi took over as head coach in 1959, the Green Bay Packers had just come off their worst season ever, with only one win all season. Most people were hoping for a more experienced coach with a reputation for turning losing teams around, not a rookie whose only head coach experience was in high school stadiums.

You wouldn't know it by the way Vince Lombardi carried himself. He quickly made it clear that he was in charge and had no intention of coaching a losing team. He implemented an unusually tough regime during his training camps, demanding absolute loyalty, dedication, and effort from his players. Those who got on board with his vision trusted him completely. They realized that he worked as hard as they did and truly believed in their potential to become a winning team.

He implemented what became the hallmark of his coaching style: simplicity and execution. He didn't have thousands of plays in his repertoire that he tried to teach his players. He wasn't a fan of unnecessary risks, fancy plays, or complicated game plans. Instead, he learned what his players did well and repeatedly practiced those plays until they could execute them perfectly. Mental toughness, hard work, consistency, and accuracy were the hallmarks of his style.

Doing fewer things but doing them better than any other team out there proved to be the winning combination, as he turned the team's losing streak around in their first season. He was named NFL Coach of the Year in his rookie season as a head coach.[4] The "Packer Sweep" became the team's signature play, and his players executed it so well that it was often successful, even when the other team knew it was coming.[3]

His single-minded determination to make winners out of a group of players who were fresh off a decade-long losing streak required confidence, determination, dedication, resilience, and a lot of mental toughness and grit. It also required having big goals and a plan to achieve them.

Goal setting

Vince Lombardi was known for doing everything methodically. Every coaching decision was deliberate, always acting with the end in mind. He set goals and milestones for himself, his players, and the team and then put his efforts where they would yield the most effective results. Setting goals and tracking performance is an excellent way to build discipline, perseverance, and grit in any aspect of life. Here are two widely used goal-setting methods to try for yourself and a tried-and-true management technique.

Objectives and Key Results (OKRs)

Objectives and Key Results (OKR) is a framework frequently used in business to define or set objectives and then the metrics by which the results will be measured. The basic format is "I/We will _____ as measured by _________."

Objectives: An objective is what you want to achieve. It should be concrete, specific, action-oriented, and significant. You should think big! Objectives are the stuff of big dreams, like landing the big promotion you've been eyeing at work.

Key Results: These are the milestones by which you will judge your ongoing progress. Objectives are what you want to do, and key results are how you are going to do it.

These are the smaller, more manageable steps along the way that will build over time to make your big dream come true. To get a promotion, there are steps you can take to improve your chances, such as updating relevant skills or having excellent performance reviews. Each step on that path is a Key Result.

When they are all accomplished, you will have met your objective. Key results are not generic and should be specific, time-bound, and measurable.[5]

New research shows that an increasing number of companies are using OKRs not just for organizational goals but also to encourage professional learning and personal development among employees. When employees are actively engaged in their own personal and professional development, the benefits tend to extend to the company as well.[6]

<u>Wish, Outcome, Obstacle, Plan (WOOP)</u>

Wish, Outcome, Obstacle, Plan (WOOP) is a realistic approach to goal setting and achievement. It focuses on your inner obstacles to reaching your dreams and helps you overcome them rather than focusing on outside barriers.

Wish: This is what you want to accomplish. Choose a slightly intimidating goal that would make a big difference in your life but that you know you need a plan to achieve. Maybe you have always wanted to take a year-long sabbatical to live in another country. That takes planning.

Outcome: In this framework, imagining the outcome goes beyond the goal itself. It examines how reaching the desired outcome will change and enhance your life. Learning a new language and immersing yourself in a new culture and way of life are benefits that extend beyond the physical act of traveling to another country.

Obstacles: Identify the internal obstacles that are most likely to get in the way of your success. If you struggle to follow through on goals even when everything is seemingly in place for success, this step may make all the difference. Perhaps you know that you will allow intrusive thoughts about losing your job and going broke to derail your plans, or you will not follow through on the savings plan you set out for yourself. What can you do to overcome your own tendency to sabotage success?

Plan: This is where you get real about how you will overcome that obstacle to make your wish come true. What are you going to do differently this time not to get sucked into the same cycle you've seen in the past? Create a plan to avoid those traps. The more detailed the plan, the better the chance of success!

Pareto Principle

Pareto Principle is not a goal-setting tool but is an excellent tool for setting priorities and managing your time. This is all about doing less and achieving more, helping you reach your goals. In a nutshell, it is the idea that around 80% of our results come from 20% of our efforts, so we focus our efforts on that 20%. More bang for your buck, so to speak.

The idea here is definitely to work smarter. It's figuring out where to focus your time, energy, and attention for the most effective results. By considering this ratio in your goal setting, you will be able to create an approach to reaching those goals that provide the results you're looking for in the most efficient and effective way possible. Vince Lombardi was famous for this. One rival coach famously remarked that Lombardi's team didn't surprise their opponents with anything complicated; they just beat them.[4]

Applying this principle to any aspect of your life will help you be more productive overall and can even be used to eliminate unnecessary items and activities. Identifying those tasks and goals that are both important and impactful will help filter out time-consuming tasks that may appear urgent but ultimately are unimportant to accomplishing your goals.

Perhaps you are trying to eat healthier, but you have found it too complicated and time-consuming to meal plan, purchase, and prepare three healthy meals a day. Not to mention, you miss your snacks! Using the Pareto Principle, this could become much simpler. Remember, the 80/20 principle is approximate, not a set-in-stone ratio. Adapt it to your needs.

Perhaps choose a rotation of the same 4 breakfasts, lunches, and dinners weekly, and eat those 5 days a week. Allow for roughly 20%, or the remaining two days of the week, to be spontaneous meals depending on what you crave. Do the same for snacks. Your meal prep gets easier, your grocery budget comes under control, and your goal of eating healthier is accomplished.

<u>Personal mission statement</u>

Have you ever noticed that large corporations and other organizations often have a mission statement? Something that defines what they are about and that keeps them focused as an organization?

Just like a corporate mission statement, a personal mission statement helps define the direction of your life. It outlines what you stand for and your values. In short, it describes your "why." A personal mission statement makes goal-setting easier, and having the resilience to continue pursuing those goals through life's inevitable setbacks will be more important than ever.

It should be no more than two to three sentences long and embody only the essentials to be effective. It should be written in positive language and clearly express what you stand for rather than what you don't. Your personal mission statement should be powerful.

First, take some time to really define who you are, who you would like to become, and the legacy you want to leave while formulating your personal mission statement. What are the values by which you live your life? What do you stand for? What legacy do you want to leave when you're gone?

A mission statement should be dynamic, so consider revisiting it regularly to ensure it accurately reflects your values and vision. Writing the statement is the first step. Living it is more important. Here are a few examples to get you started:

"To be a positive influence in all areas of life. I will focus on building a loving family and be a caring husband and father."

"To create personal happiness by focusing on the present rather than dwelling on the past. I will work on taking responsibility for creating the happiness I seek." [7]

The keys to personal growth

Lombardi's coaching career spanned from the late 1950s to the late 1960s, during which he achieved remarkable success as the head coach of the Green Bay Packers. In a single decade, he cemented his reputation as one of the best of all time.

He left Green Bay and had just led the Washington Redskins to their first winning season in 14 years when he was diagnosed with an aggressive form of colon cancer in June 1970. He died ten weeks later, before the start of the next football season.[3]

Lombardi's leadership style was rooted in a strict adherence to fundamentals and a belief in the power of teamwork. He expected his players to display unwavering commitment and self-discipline both on and off the field. Lombardi instilled a sense of accountability and demanded the highest level of effort from every player, and in return, he gave his players the best he had. It wasn't magic, and he would probably admit that it wasn't even down to exceptional talent. It was hard work, discipline, habit, and repetition, with an unwavering focus on the ultimate prize.

When Vince Lombardi died, he had the highest winning percentage of all time. More than 50 years later, he ranks third all-time despite only having coached for a decade.[8] His impact on the game was so profound that the trophy players raise over their heads after winning the Super

Bowl today is named after him: the Vince Lombardi Trophy.[4]

Action Steps

1. Set Some Goals. First, decide what you want to accomplish, then choose the goal-setting (OKR or WOOP) and tracking method you feel best suits your needs. Then, make a plan for completing them using indicators or milestones along the way.

2. Employ the KISS Method. KISS refers to Keep It Simple, Stupid.[9] We often procrastinate or put off starting something because we have made it more complicated in our minds than it has to be in reality. Let's say you want to get in shape. You don't need to start with a gym membership, personal trainer, and extremely restrictive diet. You can start simply, by making some changes to how you eat and move, which will set you on the path to better health. You can add the rest over time.

Vince Lombardi cemented his reputation as one of the best coaches the game of football has ever seen in just a few short years; his name continues to be synonymous with simplicity and flawless execution, goal-setting, hard work, drive, and excellence. From excellence on the field to excellence in the field of business, Chapter 9 shifts attention to a female entrepreneur changing the shapewear game and empowering women along the way.

Chapter Summary

- Under Lombardi's leadership, the Packers experienced their most successful period, winning five NFL Championships in the 1960s, including the first two Super Bowls.
- His leadership style was rooted in a strict adherence to fundamentals and a belief in the power of teamwork. He expected his players to display unwavering commitment and self-discipline and demanded the highest level of effort from every player.
- The belief that winning is a habit and results from every action that led up to the win was exemplified in his no-quit attitude and his famous quote, "Winners never quit, and quitters never win."
- Setting and sticking to goals built accountability and provided a clear way to measure progress. He understood the power of discipline in personal growth, including good habits, a strong work ethic, and staying committed to one's goals and values.
- Lombardi recognized the importance of mastering the fundamentals. Success starts with a solid foundation, and focusing on the basics and continuously honing one's skills is key to personal growth and achieving long-term success.

9

SARA BLAKELY

HOW TO BUILD A BILLION-DOLLAR DREAM - FAIL
ONCE A WEEK, WALK INTO THE BOARDROOM
WITH UNWAVERING RESOLVE, AND CHART THE
BOLD FUTURE YOU ENVISION WITH SARA
BLAKELY

An unflattering pair of pants and a modified pair of control-top pantyhose were the catalysts for creating SPANX, Inc., now a multimillion-dollar enterprise that sells its products in over 50 countries worldwide.

In 1998, Sara Blakely, frustrated at the way her backside looked in a pair of white pants, took matters into her own hands by wearing a pair of control top pantyhose underneath, modifying them by cutting the feet off the bottom.

A multimillion-dollar idea was born.

Despite having zero experience in the fashion industry or in running a retail business, she couldn't get the idea of creating a line of footless body-contouring pantyhose out of her head. Rather than brushing it off as a farfetched idea that would go nowhere, she focused on making it happen.

Just two years later, in 2000, she secured a factory to produce her first product, and in the same year, booked her very first order with Neiman Marcus. SPANX even made it to Oprah's Favorite Things list that same year.[1]

Sara's success moved at breakneck speed. Rather than relying on the same product to bring success year after year, Sara began expanding her product line in 2001, starting with control top fishnets. Since then, SPANX has expanded its offering to include control top underwear, maternity wear, intimates, and haute couture shapewear. Realizing that a huge demographic was untapped, SPANX launched a line of compression undershirts for men in 2010. They have since expanded into clothing as well.

The rest is history.

By 2012, she was named the world's youngest female self-made billionaire by Forbes and was also named one of Time Magazine's most influential people.[1] All this quick success is even more impressive considering the company did not open its own independent store until 2012 or launch an advertising campaign for its products until 2016.

Today, Sara Blakely is a successful entrepreneur known for founding the popular shapewear company SPANX. Her innovative approach to women's undergarments and her determination to disrupt the industry with her products have made her a prominent figure and a source of inspiration for aspiring business owners.

Entrepreneurial spirit: The creation of SPANX

As a child, Blakely's father encouraged his children to fail. It was a lesson in being fearless and in personal growth. Each week, he would ask what she had failed at that week. He would be disappointed if she hadn't failed at anything.[2] Over time, this developed into her particular brand of mental toughness. She grew to understand that failure was nothing to fear. Trying and failing at something isn't really failure. It allows you to learn from your mistakes. The real failure is to not even have the courage to try. She approached her business with that same mindset.

The founding of SPANX provided multiple opportunities to learn from failure. Sara Blakely had no prior experience in the fashion or retail industry. This lack of knowledge presented a steep learning curve as she had to navigate through unfamiliar territory and understand the intricacies of product development, manufacturing, and distribution. In one interview, she revealed that if she could go back and do something differently she would have done a better job of due diligence with key manufacturers, as one of her biggest manufacturers shut down with only four days' notice for her to find a solution.[2]

She took an idea and figured out how to build a business around it. Traditionally, entrepreneurs study business before attempting to launch a brand-new product requiring manufacturing and distribution networks to succeed. In a predominantly male-dominated industry, Sara Blakely faced gender bias and skepticism. She encountered challenges in being taken seriously as a female entrepreneur and had to assert herself and her vision with confidence and determination.[3]

Business strategies and success

Blakely's original idea was geared specifically for the female market in a way that had not been done in the past. SPANX proposed a unique product compared to available shapewear options. Blakely focused on creating seamless figure-enhancing undergarments that were, first and foremost, comfortable for women to wear all day, setting SPANX apart from traditional shapewear brands and giving it a competitive edge.

Blakely placed a strong emphasis on maintaining high product quality standards. She invested in top-notch manufacturing processes and quality control measures to ensure that each SPANX product met the most discerning customers' expectations. As a result, she quickly found fans among celebrities such as Oprah Winfrey and Gwyneth Paltrow.

Building on the success of the original line, Blakely expanded SPANX into various additional clothing categories, reaching a broader customer base and capitalizing on market trends.

Referring to herself as more of a renegade than a realist, she used a lesson her father taught her in childhood to keep going even when facing repeated rejections. To keep moving forward with her vision, she required a large amount of self-confidence and a way to banish the negative self-talk that often creeps into our minds uninvited.

Self-confidence: Transforming negative self-talk

To open up the mental space to focus on developing self-confidence, we must first work on diminishing our internal negative self-talk. Rather than being directed at others, negative self-talk refers to our inner dialogue or thoughts about ourselves. It can be difficult to overcome because we personally create and validate our beliefs about ourselves. Rather than being constructive, it negatively influences how we feel about ourselves.

Sara Blakely faced almost two years of constant rejection before being able to move forward successfully with her business. She was rejected by multiple manufacturers for being unknown in business and having almost no outside financial backing. Luckily, she already had over a decade of experience managing failure under her belt that she could call on!

She failed the LSAT, the exam needed for law school, twice. She failed at stand-up comedy. And she failed daily during her almost decade-long job as a fax-machine salesperson. However, within those failures she picked up some tools for success. Many of the most relevant ones to her SPANX business came from her time as a salesperson.

Sara believes that when cold-calling potential clients, you only have about 15 seconds to grab their attention. If you can make them smile or connect somehow, you gain another 30 seconds if you're lucky. As a result, she learned how to craft a concise but compelling sales-pitch, infusing humor into it starting with the name of the company. She also learned that face-to-face sales pitches are often more successful than phone ones, so she went out and knocked on the doors of manufacturing companies, often being told that her idea was crazy and would never sell.[4]

She admits that it wasn't always easy to not let the opinions of others affect her belief in herself and her business. She had to ensure that her inner self-talk remained positive. For many people, their inner critics would have convinced them that maybe their business idea wasn't that great, allowing their internal monologue to become negative self-talk.

<u>Reframing negative self-talk</u>

Reframing negative self-talk can be difficult because it can be hard to be objective about ourselves. It starts with becoming aware of our inner voice and questioning what it is telling us.

Two simple but powerful questions to ask when you find yourself engaging in negative self-talk:

1. *Where is the evidence that what I'm telling myself is true?*
2. *Where's the evidence that maybe it's not?*

Negative self-talk isn't always based on facts. Instead, it can be a combination of facts, our personal insecurities, and self-criticism. Watch out in particular for all-or-nothing statements like "I'm so bad with money. I'm never going to get out of debt" or "Who would want to hire me? I have no employable skills. I will never find a full-time job and have a fulfilling career." Terms like always, never, no one, or everyone rarely hold up to scrutiny.

When we accurately identify the insecurity or emotion behind the statement, we can change the narrative. Acknowledging the emotion can be enough to take some of the power away from the negative statement. That doesn't mean replacing a negative thought with a completely positive one.

That's because while sometimes our insecurities or worries are unfounded, they are based on real concerns. Pretending they aren't real and sugar-coating them in meaningless positive language can be unhelpful. We want to begin conditioning ourselves to have honest, realistic thoughts that are as free from judgment or unrealistic statements as possible.

Try reframing your statements to reflect the feelings behind them more accurately. "I'm so far in debt I'm *terrified* that I'll never get out. I need to improve my money management habits." "It's been so long since I've had a full-time job that I'm *afraid* my skills are all outdated. If I don't update them, I'm *worried* that I will never have a fulfilling career."

Neither of these new statements ignores the very real concerns behind them, nor do they offer unhelpful platitudes couched in overly positive language. Instead, they both a) identify the main concern, b) identify the emotion involved, and c) indicate the actionable area to be addressed.

In the first statement, the concern is getting out of debt. The emotion is fear. The action area is improving money management skills. In the second statement, the concern is finding full-time work. The emotion is worry. The action area is updating job skills. By evaluating your negative self-talk in this manner, you can identify whether your thought is accurate and reframe it in a way that allows you to take action to make a change.

Managing emotions and stress

Sara also managed her emotions and stress as she faced countless rejections for her product. She relied on self-regulation and resilience to see her through.

As a child, she witnessed a horrific accident in which a friend was run over and killed, her father gave her a gift of a series on tape called *How To Be A No-Limit Person*,[5] which focused on living your life to the fullest while dealing with life's many frustrations, as well as how to separate yourself from external criticism. She credits it with completely changing her outlook on life.

Taking control of your emotions through self-regulation is one of the best ways to ensure that you don't make decisions out of anger, fear, or any other emotion that crowds out judgment. This is where self-control comes into play. You may be angry, but you are responsible for your response. When you are able to self-regulate, you are more conscientious, adaptable, and trustworthy.

While no one can completely control their circumstances, mentally tough individuals strive to control their reactions to life's obstacles. Mastering control over your emotions means that you choose the response to a difficult scenario rather than allowing a temporary emotion to get in the way of the best solution. Mentally tough people analyze their emotions and then channel them constructively to control their responses rather than letting them control them.

Consider the ABC Model often employed in cognitive behavioral therapy practice. A is the trigger, or event. C is the consequence of the event.[6] Many people believe that A causes C. Let's look at two examples:

- A-Someone cuts you off in traffic, causing you to,
- C-Become angry and honk your horn repeatedly, yelling at them out the window.
- A-You get overlooked for a role in the play, so
- C-Obviously you are a terrible actor and decide to give up your dream of acting.

The key to managing emotions and ultimately one's reactions is by recognizing that it is not A that causes C, but B, your belief. Let's look at the above examples again.

- A-Someone cuts you off in traffic.
- B- You feel a flash of anger, but realize that road rage is not going to solve the problem.
- C-You shake it off and let it go.
- A-You are overlooked for a role in the play.
- B-You are disappointed but understand that rejection is part of the business.
- C-You ask the director for feedback and commit to working on your acting while applying for different roles.

Newer versions of the model add an additional D, and E, which stand for Disputing an irrational belief to turn it into a rational one, which results in a new Effect as a consequence. Theorists argue that D and E are already present in the original model, but have simply been made more explicitly obvious in the expanded model. For example, in the first example above:

- A-Someone cuts you off in traffic.
- B-You start thinking: *They are so inconsiderate! They don't care about anyone else on the road. I can't believe this! This always happens to me!*
- C-You feel angry, frustrated, and helpless.
- D-You question your thoughts: *Are they really inconsiderate, or could they just be distracted or in a*

hurry? Does this really always happen to me, or is this just a single incident?

- E-You shake it off and let it go.

In the second example:

- A-You are overlooked for a role in the play.
- B-You are disappointed and start thinking: *I prepared so much for this. Maybe I'm not good enough. I'll never get any good roles.*
- C-You feel discouraged and about to head home.
- D-However, you start asking yourself: *Is it really true that not getting this role means I'm a failure? There are many reasons why a director might choose someone else.*
- E-You go back and ask the director for feedback and commit to working on your acting while applying for different roles.

<u>Red backpack</u>

Sara is known for her iconic red backpack and its role in her first big break. When she was struggling with constant rejections while trying to launch her business, she decided that she needed to have her "lucky" red backpack that she had used throughout college. She started carrying the backpack everywhere, including sales pitches, including the one at Neiman Marcus that landed her first sale.

By choosing an object that brought her mentally back to a time in her life when she felt confident and powerful, Sara

Blakely was able to draw on that feeling when facing an uncertain future. Now, every woman who benefits from her foundation's grants also receives a red backpack, as a symbol of their potential.

Philanthropy and empowerment

Sara Blakely has used her success in business to support other women. The company's mission statement is: To help women feel great about themselves and their potential. Blakely backs that up with action in her philanthropic endeavors.

In 2013, she became the first female billionaire to sign the Giving Pledge—the movement started in 2010 by Bill Gates, Melinda French Gates, and Warren Buffet that invites billionaires to pledge to give at least 50% of their wealth to charity, either within their lifetimes or in their wills. Individuals can choose where to donate the money, and Sara has pledged her money to empower underserved women, such as those living in poverty.[7]

At the time of her pledge, her foundation, the SPANX by Sara Blakely Foundation, had already donated over $20 million to charities that support women and girls, including a $1 million donation to the Oprah Winfrey Leadership Academy Foundation in South Africa.[1]

Blakely established The Sara Blakely Foundation in 2006, focusing on supporting and empowering women. The foundation's mission is to provide women with the resources and opportunities they need to reach their full potential. It supports organizations that offer education, entrepreneurship, and empowerment programs for women and girls.

The SPANX by Sara Blakely Foundation is an extension of her commitment to female empowerment via partnerships with other organizations. Through this foundation, she supports women-owned small businesses. Blakely collaborates with non-profit organizations that align with her mission of empowering women. She has partnered with organizations like Girls Inc., Vital Voices, and Dress for Success, providing financial support and mentorship opportunities.

Most recently, her foundation teamed up with GlobalGiving to create the Red Backpack Fund, which donated $5 million to support female entrepreneurs in the wake of the COVID-19 pandemic. GlobalGiving managed the funds, giving out 1000 grants of $5000 to female entrepreneurs in the United States.[8]

Action Steps

1. Turn Around Negative Self-Talk. We are often unaware of how often negative thoughts about ourselves pass through our minds. Keep a one-day list of all the negative self-talk you recognize. At the end of the day, rewrite those thoughts to be more realistic. *Follow the formula:*

1. Identify the concern. *"I'm failing my courses."*

2. Identify the emotion. *"I'm too stupid to complete my degree" could be reframed as "I'm **worried** that I will have to drop out of school."*
3. Include one actionable item. *"I can go to the university student support center twice weekly for tutoring and support."*

2. Find Your Red Backpack. Sara used a red backpack as a good luck charm and reminder of her belief in herself and her business idea and has passed on that tradition in her philanthropic endeavors. What object, mantra, or ritual would give you that extra confidence when facing something difficult?

Sara Blakely took an idea, allowed herself to dream, and then turned her dream into a reality through sheer force of will, perseverance, and hard work. In Chapter 10, we turn our focus to South Africa and one of the most iconic activists and leaders in the country's history, Nelson Mandela, whose mental toughness and steadfast resilience helped him through 27 years of imprisonment.

Chapter Summary

- Sara Blakely broke into a male-dominated industry as an entrepreneur with no experience in the fashion industry with the creation of SPANX. She went on to build a shapewear empire.

- Her self-confidence and resilience helped her succeed despite facing gender bias and skepticism in a competitive retail landscape.
- Don't be afraid of failure. She applied her father's childhood lesson to her business ethic, preferring to try and fail rather than not try at all. After facing multiple rejections, Blakely worked on managing her emotions, self-talk, and stress levels.
- SPANX was a unique product created and marketed directly to women, focusing on quality, comfort, and top-notch materials and construction. The product's reputation helped garner a thriving consumer base, allowing her to expand her company's product offerings over time successfully.
- The Sara Blakely Foundation focuses on supporting and empowering women to provide other women with the resources and opportunities they need to reach their full potential. It supports organizations that offer education, entrepreneurship, and empowerment programs for women and girls.
- SPANX by Sara Blakely Foundation is an extension of her commitment to female empowerment, supporting women-owned small businesses.

10

NELSON MANDELA

27 YEARS AND ONE UNBROKEN SPIRIT - HOW
NELSON MANDELA'S CONVICTION AND
COMMITMENT TO THE CAUSE THAT BRIDGED
DIVIDES CAN INSPIRE YOU TO TRANSFORM THE
WORLD

In 1994, Nelson Mandela became the first black president of South Africa, as well as the first fully democratically elected president. During his historic five-year term, he guided his country through a series of monumental changes that forever altered the trajectory of the former apartheid nation. Elected just four years after being released from 27 years of imprisonment for his beliefs and acts of resistance against the government, he took control of a newly desegregated South Africa at the age of 77.[1] In 1999, he refused to run for a second term, and retired from politics, despite an 80% approval rating.[2]

The road to the presidency, however historic, was almost impossible.

A political prisoner for 27 years for his part in the armed resistance against the white-run apartheid government of South Africa, Nelson Mandela remained a symbol of the resistance for almost three decades during his imprisonment, despite his words being banned in the country.[3]

Rather than be broken by his experience in prison, he emerged as a unifying and transformative figure who helped guide his country through a difficult transition period. His story of resilience and how he managed stress and developed positive habits while imprisoned is a great testament to his incredible mental toughness.

Upon his release from prison in 1990, which was broadcast worldwide, he gave a speech to the press reconfirming his commitment to peace and reconciliation, but also unapologetically declaring that the armed struggle was not over and would continue for as long as necessary to win equal rights for non-white South Africans.[4]

He then spent the next several years negotiating an end to the apartheid regime, engaging international support, and working for peace in South Africa. Alongside the President at the time, F.W. de Klerk, he helped negotiate a transition to a one-person, one-vote electoral system, all while ensuring a peaceful transition to the end of apartheid. Mandela and de Klerk were joint recipients of the Nobel Peace Prize in 1993 for their incredible efforts to transform South Africa.[5]

Apartheid

Apartheid, which means "apartness" in Afrikaans, was literally used to separate or keep different racial and ethnic groups apart, enforced by law. South Africa was governed under apartheid from May 1948 until May 1994. One racial group, in this case black South Africans, is deprived of their rights and treated inferior to another group, namely white South Africans. White South Africans held complete political power, upholding and enforcing laws that discriminated against, for the most part, black South African citizens.

In 1950, South African citizens were officially classified as Bantu (Black), Colored (Mixed race), or White. A fourth category of Asian (mainly Indian and Pakistani) was added later. One's official category determined one's rights, including where one could live and work.[6] Some of the more damaging laws:

- Made interracial relationships and marriages illegal.
- Classified areas for living, owning businesses, or owning land as white-only.
- The Land Acts of 1954 and 1955 completed a process begun much earlier that designated 80% of the country's land for whites, despite white citizens making up less than 20% of the country's population.
- Non-white citizens were required to carry

documentation authorizing their presence in restricted areas.

- People were forced to leave their homes to live in townships outside of white areas according to their registered race. However, land ownership was forbidden to non-whites and so many people lost their homes and their land and were forced to rent instead.
- Schools were segregated, with non-white schools focusing on preparing students for manual labor or the "menial" labor the government thought they were suited for.
- National universities were discouraged from accepting non-white students.
- Black South Africans lost all political rights in 1970, as they were forcibly reclassified as citizens of segregated "Bantu Homelands" that were granted autonomous rule on paper but not in practice.
- To keep the system in place and stop any unrest, it was illegal to protest the government.[6]

Activism, imprisonment, and commitment to the cause

<u>Activism</u>

The man the world knows as Nelson Mandela was born Rolihlahla Mandela in South Africa in 1918. The name Nelson was given to him when he started school, following the tradition at the time of teachers giving students "Christian" names rather than calling them by the names given by their parents. He continued to use the name into adulthood.[7] A strong student, he was accepted into one of the best universities for black South Africans. He was always aware of the injustices taking place in his country; however, the first time he suffered a serious consequence for his activism was when he was expelled from university for joining a student protest.

Still, he did not commit himself fully to the cause until the 1940s, becoming a member of the African National Congress (ANC), a Black-liberation group, in 1942. He then helped to form the Youth League wing of the organization. The goal was to help organize the peasants and laborers who traditionally did not have a voice, using a different type of protest than the ANC's traditional method of "polite" protest against the government, which the Youth wing found ineffective. Instead, they used civil disobedience, boycotts, non-cooperation, and strikes, with the express goals of land redistribution, free education, and full citizenship, among others.[4]

Nelson Mandela's willingness to risk his livelihood and well-being by holding illegal government protests for the good of others is an example of courage in the midst of a very difficult situation.

<u>Militancy</u>

In the early 1950s, Mandela began participating in more overtly defiant actions against government policies as the leader of the Defiance Campaign. He was jailed in 1952, along with over 8,000 others, for participating in actions such as deliberately violating curfew laws and refusing to carry identification passes. He was put on trial for treason in 1956, and acquitted in 1961.[3]

That didn't stop him from doubling down on his commitment to the cause, and in fact, only served to increase his conviction that moving from peaceful to more violent protest was the only way forward. He was on the path to becoming one of the leaders of the armed resistance against the South African government.

<u>Guerilla Warfare</u>

His conviction and commitment to the cause of a unified South Africa free from apartheid was an ideal for which he was prepared to die. In 1960, government forces killed 69 black protesters in the town of Sharpeville and subsequently banned the ANC. As it went underground, a militant wing emerged.

Nelson Mandela turned his focus to armed resistance and became the leader of that militant branch, the Umkhonto we Sizwe or MK for short. It means Spear of the Nation, to represent the traditional African weapon that had been used to resist white incursions in the past. He recruited members of all races to the group who shared the same long-term goals, breaking away from the black-only membership policy of the ANC.[8]

In June 1961, he released a letter to the nation urging the people to join him in the resistance, asking them to choose between action and complicity, between raising their voices for freedom or remaining silent and neutral in matters of life and death. He acknowledged the arrest warrant against him, and reiterated his commitment to fighting for the freedom of all South Africans until his final day.[9]

Determination, discipline, and an unbreakable spirit

In 1964, Nelson Mandela was convicted of sabotage and treason, and sentenced to life in prison. The conditions of his imprisonment were harsh. In the beginning, he could only send and receive one letter every six months, as well as meet one visitor for 30 minutes.

For 18 of his 27 years of imprisonment, Mandela was imprisoned on Robben Island, along with eight other ANC members. The small group of prisoners were completely isolated from the outside world, and forced to work long, grueling hours in the quarry, pounding rocks into gravel.

There were no white prisoners in the maximum-security compound, and the black prisoners were treated worse than prisoners of other non-white racial groups. Conditions were engineered specifically to break the resolve of Mandela and the other political prisoners, who were kept in a separate section from other prisoners.

They were forced to wear shorts and sandals year-round, while other prisoners could wear pants and closed shoes in winter. They were fed less than their Asian, Indian, or mixed-race counterparts. They were not allowed to have desks in their cells, or to read or study.[10,11]

Cultivating mental toughness and advocating for change from a prison cell

Rather than breaking Nelson Mandela down, the unfair circumstances induced him to use his mental toughness to strengthen his resolve. He decided to organize his fellow political prisoners to advocate for better conditions in prison, starting with granting black prisoners access to the same conditions as the others.

Even in a place bereft of almost all freedoms, Mandela was able to fight for equal access to the few freedoms there were. Eventually, they were successful, and the prison changed. Black prisoners were granted the right to wear long pants in winter, have desks in their cells, read, study, and even plant a garden. Prisoners were granted permission to organize sporting events and to listen to music.[10] These changes boosted the morale of all prisoners and reminded Mandela and others that positive change was possible.

While he was temporarily unable to participate in the larger struggle for equality in South Africa as a free man, Mandela viewed the conditions in prison as a microcosm of society as a whole. By fighting for improved conditions inside jail, he felt he was contributing to the larger cause in the way that was available to him at the time. It helped him stay mentally strong and gave him something to focus on, that ultimately served a bigger purpose. Rather than being a victim of circumstance, he focused on growing his circle of influence.

In 2015, the United Nations updated the Standard Minimum Rules for the Treatment of Prisoners that had initially been adopted in 1955. In doing so, they took inspiration from Nelson Mandela's civil disobedience movement while he was imprisoned, which led to improved conditions at Robben Island Prison. The expanded set of rules is known as the Nelson Mandela Rules.[12] His influence continued even after his death.

Circle of concern, influence, and control

Mentally tough individuals are proactive. They focus on what they can do, not on what they can't. The ancient Stoic philosophers believed that humans had a circle of control, which included mostly those things that dealt with our inner lives, and that we should focus our efforts there. We may be concerned about other things, our circle of concern, but we have no control over them. Modern-day philosophers and therapists have expanded upon these ideas by adding a third circle, the circle of influence.[12] Let's look at each more closely below, starting with the outermost circle and moving our way in.

Circle of concern

Your circle of concern includes things you are concerned or worried about, but that you currently have no influence over. Spending your time being upset about what you cannot control can lead to feeling like a victim of your circumstances, and makes it easier to do nothing at all since it all seems pointless. Some examples of things that may be in your circle of concern are other people's thoughts and actions, the economy, the weather, or world peace.

Nelson Mandela's circle of concern included, among other things, an end to the apartheid system in South Africa, equality and freedom for all South Africans, and improved conditions for prisoners.

Circle of influence

Moving inward is the circle of influence. This is a relatively new concept, as it sits somewhere between what you can and cannot control, a gray zone. This is where you do have some ability to influence. In some cases your circle of influence can grow, eventually encompassing some items that were formerly only within your circle of concern.

While incarcerated, Nelson Mandela worked on his circle of influence in different ways. He committed to educating both prisoners and guards about his vision of freedom and equality for all South Africans. He chose to organize prisoners to advocate for better conditions for all inmates, including coordinating civil disobedience actions.

His steadfastness and refusal to succumb to the harsh prison conditions actually helped to widen his circle of influence outside of prison, where the story of his unjust imprisonment galvanized the fight for freedom and a unified South Africa. However, it is important to keep in mind that your circle of influence is still in many ways out of your direct control.

Circle of control

This is the one circle in which you actually have direct control over change. It is concerned specifically with your inner life. It includes things such as emotions, beliefs, and reactions to things that happen to us in life. We cannot always control what happens, but we can control our reactions and our behavior. Those who focus on their circle of control tend to be more resilient and express higher levels of subjective well-being.

Nelson Mandela focused on his circle of control in prison by focusing on his physical and mental wellbeing, and by working on his own personal growth and transformation. He dedicated himself to staying physically fit, to studying, and to educating his fellow prisoners and prison guards. [14] [15]

Personal growth and transformation

In the restrictive environment of prison, Nelson Mandela maintained a disciplined daily routine. This included exercising, reading, and engaging in political discussions with fellow prisoners. Establishing and adhering to a routine provided structure and stability during challenging times.

Physical discipline

He used the little free time available to him to focus on personal growth and transformation. He also used his disciplined daily routine as a way to stay physically fit, to keep his mind healthy and strong, and to battle the monotony of prison life. Nelson Mandela had a strict exercise regimen he followed before imprisonment, and he made a conscious choice to adapt it to his circumstances in jail, despite already working several hours a day in the quarry pounding rocks into gravel.

As a result, he started his day at 5:00 a.m. Monday to Thursday, getting in a full workout in a prison cell just over two meters squared, before having to perform several more hours of grueling manual labor. His workout was impressive and demonstrated the no-excuses attitude that discipline demands: 45 minutes of running on the spot, 100 fingertip pushups, 200 sit-ups, 50 deep knee bends, and a variety of calisthenic exercises. In later interviews, he attributed his daily exercise regimen in prison as helping him survive the ordeal, as it provided him an outlet for his frustrations. It was a habit he maintained his entire life, believing strongly that a fit body helped him work better and kept his mind clear. [13]

Mental transformation

Nelson Mandela also used his time in prison to transform himself mentally. Surviving prison, particularly in the conditions in which Mandela was kept and for the length of time he served, requires a measure of resilience, self-control, and mental toughness beyond what the average person develops in a lifetime.

Rather than succumbing to depression, anger, or thoughts of revenge, Nelson Mandela emerged from prison a calm, self-reflective, and influential leader. He found that in prison he had more time to sit and think about himself, his past, the realities of the struggle, and the shape he hoped the future to take than ever before. He identified his personal weaknesses and worked on improving them. Although he is known for his role in changing the course of an entire nation, he felt that the most difficult task in life is changing oneself.[15]

He developed the view that prison itself was a microcosm of South African society. He took very seriously the opportunity to better understand not only his fellow prisoners from different backgrounds, but the guards as well. The time spent speaking with, learning from, and bringing together prisoners and guards from different backgrounds helped refine his view of how a unified South Africa could work. It also helped sharpen his negotiating skills, which were essential to him upon his release from prison.[14]

Rather than succumbing to the temptation to view himself as a victim of circumstance, Mandela found a way to make meaning of his time in prison by working on himself both physically and mentally. He never gave in to the frustration and anger that could have so easily consumed him, instead choosing to control that which was within his reach, including his reactions to some of the most difficult situations imaginable.

Action Steps

1. Routine & Structure. Think about your own daily routine. Is it a routine that you designed to best serve you and your goals? Or do you feel like "life" is too unpredictable or pulls you in several directions at once? Keep a log of your daily activities for one week. Then identify the times when you can impose your own routine and structure, and then put together a weekly schedule that gives you more control over your time.

2. Strategic Decision-Making. As a leader, Mandela displayed strategic thinking and disciplined decision-making. He carefully considered the consequences of his actions, making choices that aligned with the long-term goals of the anti-apartheid movement. The results you get tomorrow depend on the decisions you make today. Think about your biggest, most important long-term goals. Now think about the decisions you made the past two weeks. Did they promote your long-term goals? If not, what decisions can you make next week that are better aligned?

3. Circles of Concern, Influence, and Control. What are some issues that fall into your circle of concern? List as many as you can. Choose three of those items, and write down at least one action for each that falls within your circle of influence. Finally, list at least one action for each that falls within your circle of control.

For example, Nelson Mandela's circle of concern included the end of apartheid and equal rights for all

South African citizens. While imprisoned, his circle of influence included educating prisoners and guards about his vision, and advocating for equal prison conditions for all inmates. His circle of control included his dedication to keeping himself physically and mentally strong enough to endure the harsh conditions of his imprisonment, and choosing to put his energy toward organizing his fellow prisoners to advocate for change.

Nelson Mandela's dedication to creating a free and equal South Africa was recognized around the world, and his calm demeanor upon his release from prison belied the extreme resilience and mental toughness that helped him not only survive prison but emerge committed to unity and not anger or vengeance. In Chapter 11, we move from the oldest mentor to the youngest, in education activist Malala Yousafzai, whose incredible courage and strength have inspired a generation of girls and boys to fight for the right to go to school.

Chapter Summary

- Apartheid was the official system in South Africa from 1948 to 1994, which legally enforced segregation and racial discrimination against non-white citizens of South Africa.
- Nelson Mandela joined the African National Congress (ANC) in 1944 and became involved in resistance against the ruling apartheid government in 1948.

- In 1964, Nelson Mandela was convicted of sabotage and treason, and sentenced to life in prison. He spent the next 27 years in jail.
- Mandela developed mental toughness in prison by cultivating discipline in the form of physical fitness, using it as an outlet for stress and frustration.
- He focused on his circles of control and influence before, during, and after incarceration to affect change in an area that for decades was only within his circle of concern, the end of apartheid.

11

MALALA YOUSAFZAI

HOW CAN YOU MAKE A DIFFERENCE? -
EMBRACE THE FRESH PERSPECTIVE AND
OPTIMISM OF THE YOUTH AND SHAKE THINGS
UP FOR THE BETTER WITH MALALA YOUSAFZAI

At the young age of 11 Malala Yousafzai wrote an anonymous blog for the BBC about what it was like living under the Taliban in Pakistan.

She won Pakistan's first Youth National Peace Prize in 2011.

In 2012, she was shot in the head by the Taliban in an assassination attempt, and following treatment in Pakistan, was flown to London for additional surgery.

Just ten months later, she spoke at the United Nations Youth Assembly, delivering a message of defiance, declaring that the Taliban's goal of silencing her had failed.

In 2013, she released her first autobiographical book: *I Am Malala*. She also started her own foundation to support the education of girls worldwide.

At the age of 17, Malala Yousafzai won the Nobel Peace Prize. She was the youngest Nobel Laureate in history. She was also the first Pashtun, and first Pakistani to receive the prize.

Malala achieved more before her 18th birthday than most people do their whole lives.

And she was just getting started.

Malala Yousafzai's story highlights the ways in which mental toughness is not limited by age or sex. She displayed incredible courage, claimed agency over her message and refused to become a victim, and continued her unwavering commitment to her beliefs both before and after the life-changing attack. Her story is a reminder that mentors need not always be those older and traditionally considered wiser. Sometimes the optimism of youth and a fresh perspective are what's needed to shake things up for the better.

Early life: The rise of the Taliban

Malala was born in the Swat Valley in Pakistan in 1997. Most families in her community value the birth of baby boys over girls, and few came to congratulate her parents on her birth as a result. However, Malala's parents were thrilled at her arrival, and her father even added her birth to the all-male family tree.[1]

Malala's father was a teacher and ran a school for girls, and was determined that she would receive the same educational opportunities that Pakistani boys did. However, during Malala's early years, the Swat Valley witnessed increasing militancy and the rise of the Taliban, which led to the imposition of their version of strict Islamic laws and restrictions.

The Taliban is an ultraconservative political and religious group that emerged in Afghanistan in the aftermath of the Afghan war that ended in 1992. The word translates to "students" in the Pashto language, as most members were men studying Islam in the madrassas. (These are typically schools that offer religious education, but they are not all strictly religious. Many teach secular subjects as well.)

The group rose to fill the void left by the Afghan government in the areas outside of Kabul. Crime and corruption from local militias and warlords terrorized the citizens of Afghanistan, and the Taliban emerged as a force to combat it. Combining strict religious ideology mixed with a strict Pashtun social code, they quickly rose to power, taking control of Kabul and two-thirds of Afghanistan by late 1996.[2]

While welcomed by some, their rise to power was controversial and opposed by many within Afghanistan itself. They introduced repressive laws, including the near total exclusion of women from society, banning them from working outside the home, and banning girls from attending school. They destroyed non-Islamic monuments and implemented harsh criminal punishments for even minor crimes. In the wake of the 2001 terror attack on the World Trade Center in New York City, the Taliban refused to extradite Osama Bin Laden to the United States. The United States began military activity in Afghanistan in October of 2001, aiding in toppling the Taliban from power in December of that same year.[2]

By the time Malala was 10 years old, the Taliban had regrouped and moved into Pakistan. Pakistan was one of only three countries to have recognized Taliban rule in Afghanistan as legitimate, and they initially found a sympathetic reception in the Pashtun region of the Swat Valley. However, that was short-lived, as a campaign of terror was increasingly waged on the residents, and the bodies of decapitated policemen left in the streets became a common sight. By 2009, up to one-third of the 1.5 million population had left, many heading for the relief camps opened in the city of Mingora. What was once coined the "Switzerland of Asia" had become a war zone under Taliban rule.[1]

The Taliban imposed severe restrictions on residents, just as they had in Afghanistan. Many specifically targeted women and girls. Females were forbidden to be in public spaces without the accompaniment of a male relative, and they were banned from school and work. By 2009, Pakistani education officials reported that 173 schools had been blown up, 105 of them schools for girls.[3]

Of particular impact on Malala was the ban on girls attending school. Malala had already been speaking out about the restrictions on girls attending school, but this was the catalyst for deepening her activism, pushing for education reform in the country.

<u>Budding activism</u>

Alongside her father, she began giving interviews to local media, sharing her thoughts on the importance of education for girls and pushing for change. Despite the increased number of attacks on civilians who defied the Taliban or questioned their edicts, and the growing number of bodies in "the bloody square" left to deter further dissent, Malala never considered backing down from speaking out. Not even after her father started receiving threats of his own.

It was at this time that her father was approached by his friend who worked for the BBC, looking for a female teacher or schoolgirl to write a diary for the BBC. Malala volunteered, despite the risk. The journal was anonymous, and she was warned that if her name got out it could endanger her. She courageously chose to be a voice for the voiceless, at great personal risk.[1]

She later participated in a documentary for the *New York Times* website that included being followed by a camera as she got ready for school, defying the Taliban-imposed law banning girls from attending school. Many feared the Taliban might kill her father as retribution for her outspokenness, but few believed they would murder a child. Unfortunately, as the situation deteriorated, Malala and her family also left their home for their safety.[1]

Assassination attempt

As Malala became a household name in Pakistan and participated in an increasing number of events covered by the media, she also became a target for the Taliban. She worried about the threats her father received and understood that she was also in danger. She often imagined how an attack might happen, hoping that she would be able to initiate a conversation with a would-be attacker in order to share her thoughts first.

Unfortunately, she didn't get the chance to speak first. She was targeted while riding on a bus on her way home from school. A young man boarded the back of the bus, asked for her by name, and shot her in the head. Three bullets struck her in the head and neck, requiring immediate surgery. She was first taken to a hospital in Pakistan, where she underwent lifesaving treatment. She was then taken to England, where more surgeries took place, and where Malala underwent rehabilitation. She didn't know it at the time, but it was also where she would make her new life.[1]

Recuperation and personal growth

Despite suffering from three bullet wounds and an overseas transfer to England, Malala miraculously suffered no lasting brain or nerve damage. She was released from the hospital within three months, though has returned for multiple surgeries since.[4] As she physically recuperated, she also had to work on her mental wounds and find a way to adapt to her new reality.

She initially assumed that she would be returning to Pakistan and requested schoolbooks so that she could study for exams. However, as the Taliban publicly indicated that she would be targeted again should she return to the country, it was eventually decided that her family would stay in England. She suddenly faced adapting to a new language, culture, and school system.[5] In addition, she had become a household name worldwide, with everyone wondering about her next move.

She worked on healing herself and continuing her advocacy for education. This time, her stage was worldwide, and she expanded her focus from her home country's educational challenges to fight for the right to education for all girls around the world, first speaking at the United Nations less than a year after being attacked, to launching her foundation and autobiography in 2013.[6]

Criticism, taking control of the narrative, and courageous conversations

Criticism

In the wake of the attack, Malala's story was picked up by international news outlets, causing worldwide shock and outrage. The image of a teenage girl brutally shot at point-blank range in broad daylight brought the realities of life under Taliban rule into focus for millions of people in a way earlier reports had not always successfully done.

In contrast, in her home country, many media outlets turned against her. Some accused her father of shooting her, others questioned if she had been shot at all, and others still accused her of staging everything so she could move to a Western country and lead a more glamorous life. Social media accounts from Pakistan and surrounding countries furthered those rumors.[7]

As Malala returned to the public eye less than a year later, speaking at the United Nations and giving interviews to Western media outlets, support for her and her cause was not the only response. Many in the West and elsewhere questioned whether Malala was speaking of her own accord, or being fed what to say by the adults in her life, including her father, a well-known activist in his own right.

Many painted her as a victim of Western imperialism, being used to further justify ongoing military intervention in Pakistan, Afghanistan, and elsewhere in the region.[8] Starting in 2004, the United States began targeting Al Qaeda and Taliban militants in areas along the Afghanistan-Pakistan border, employing drones to bomb various targets. The drones did manage to kill militants, but they also killed civilians, causing backlash. As the conflict fanned out into other areas of Pakistan and Afghanistan, more civilian bloodshed followed. Estimates put the current number of civilian Pakistani deaths since 2001 at approximately 24, 099.[9]

On the surface, such criticism was leveled at the politicians and media outlets who clamored for Malala's attention, using her story as a way to turn public opinion in their favor.[8]

Below the surface, criticism of this type infantilized Malala, painting her as a naive child, taking away her agency, and discrediting her voice. It also failed to recognize that she had been an outspoken activist even before the attack, and was not simply a convenient tool to be used by adults to further their agenda. Rather than be discouraged by such criticism both at home and abroad, it steeled Malala's resolve to continue to use her voice to advocate for equal education opportunities for both girls and boys in every country worldwide.

Taking control of the narrative

One way she did that was by taking back control of the narrative. Rather than allowing herself to be painted as the victim, she displayed a strength of mind and conviction in the cause beyond her years. She understood the importance of cultivating a relationship with Western media, but pushed back on some of the narrative that was expected of her.

A proud Muslim, Malala referenced the teachings of Islam as the basis for her arguments that the education of both girls and boys was both a right and a responsibility for children of the faith. She positioned the Taliban as more of a political organization than a religious one, and insisted that retribution in the form of more military intervention was not the right approach.[8]

Rather than allowing the media to carve out an image of her as an innocent, naive pawn in a larger political game, she quietly but confidently took control of her image whenever she appeared in the media.

Courageous conversations

As Malala's influence grew, she recognized the importance of inclusivity in her advocacy work. She actively sought to include diverse perspectives and engage with a wide range of stakeholders, including policymakers, educators, parents, and grassroots activists.

She cultivated empathy and compassion for those facing injustice, which enabled her to connect in solidarity with people from various cultures, religions, and socioeconomic backgrounds.

It wasn't always easy. Malala started her foundation to help put her ideology into action in countries where education inequality exists.[6] This meant soliciting donations, initiating negotiations with high-level political figures, and keeping herself and her cause in the public eye.

Difficult conversations about important topics became a way of life. In her book, she describes her visit to the White House during the Obama administration. Upon receiving the invitation, her response was that she would attend if her visit was to be more than a simple photo opportunity. She wanted the freedom to speak her mind and share her thoughts with the President. Her wish was granted, and one of the topics they discussed was her belief that drone attacks were doing more harm than good in her country, and fueling more terrorism as a result. She encouraged the Obama administration to put more money into education instead.[1]

Action Steps

1. Courageous Conversations. Malala has used her voice to consistently have the difficult conversations around improving access to education for girls at the highest levels, including challenging the United States president on the continued use of drone attacks instead of investing in education instead. For many people, the fear of short-term discomfort or embarrassment wins out over the potential long-term benefits that can be had via courageous conversations that address uncomfortable but important issues. What courageous conversations have you been avoiding? Choose one conversation you have been putting off, and take five minutes today to schedule that conversation within the next week.

2. Take Control of the Narrative. Malala was often accused of being used as a pawn by the media to justify military action by the United States and its allies in Pakistan and the surrounding regions. She refused to allow critics to take away her agency and took control of the narrative, insisting that she be taken seriously for her personal stance. When times are tough, it is often easier to succumb to the idea that we are victims of others' opinions rather than the author of our own story. In what area of your life have you allowed someone else's version of your truth to take precedence? How can you begin to reclaim that story for your own?

Chapter Summary

- Malala Yousafzai was born in Swat Valley, Pakistan, in 1997. Her father defied tradition by adding her to the all-male family tree and declaring that she would receive the same opportunities as boys.
- In 2007, the Taliban took over control of her region, and within two years, one-third of the population had fled and 173 schools had been blown up, 105 of which were schools for girls.
- Malala continued to attend school clandestinely and began advocating for education reform to allow girls to return to school.
- In 2012, while returning home from school she was shot by the Taliban in an assassination attempt.
- Malala used her platform to advance her philanthropic work and started the Malala Foundation, advocating for equal access to education for boys and girls around the world.
- She employed determination and courage in her fight for equal rights, and turned criticism

around by taking control of the public narrative
of her life.

- She demonstrates her continued mental
toughness by using her influence to challenge
world leaders on their policies, never shying away
from having the difficult, uncomfortable
conversations that lead to change.

AFTERWORD

In the relentless pursuit of personal and professional excellence, mental toughness is an indispensable trait to cultivate on life's journey. In this book, we have been privileged to glean insights from ten exceptional mentors who have dedicated their lives to cultivating the virtues of resilience, determination, and perseverance. Mental toughness is not a static trait but a dynamic quality that can be nurtured and refined over time. The mentors featured in this exploration have served as inspirations for individuals striving to navigate the challenges of life with grace and tenacity.

One overarching theme that resonates through the narratives of these mentors is the significance of mindset. Each mentor emphasizes the power of perception and embodies a growth mindset, urging individuals to view challenges not as insurmountable obstacles but as opportunities for growth. In a world plagued by adversity, cultivating a growth mindset emerges as the linchpin for mental toughness. It is not the absence of challenges, but one's response to them that matters most.

Another recurring narrative is the acknowledgment of failure as an integral part of the journey towards mental toughness. Failure, rather than being a deterrent, is positioned as a stepping stone towards success. These mentors demonstrate the power of a paradigm shift in how we perceive setbacks. They encourage us to see them as setups for future triumphs. The ability to bounce back from failure, to extract lessons from defeat, and to persist in the face of adversity is a testament to one's mental toughness.

The mentors featured here hail from diverse backgrounds —sports, business, activism, politics, and the arts— underscoring the universality of mental toughness. Whether it's the steely resolve of Malala Yousafzai, who defied the oppressive forces of extremism to champion education for girls, or the indomitable will of Serena Williams, who, with her unparalleled success in tennis, emphasized that a strong and disciplined body is the canvas upon which her mental resilience was painted, there are lessons in each mentor's story to benefit the average person.

In celebrating these icons, we celebrate not just their achievements but the essence of the human spirit—the capacity to endure, to evolve, and to inspire. The threads that weave through their narratives—mindset, self-awareness, and embracing failure—form the fabric of mental toughness. Each narrative serves as a chapter in a collective story of triumph over adversity. They have illuminated the path for individuals from all walks of life, demonstrating that mental toughness is a journey accessible to anyone willing to make the effort to achieve it.

As we embark on our individual journeys, may we carry the lessons of these mentors' insights, using them to help guide us through life with resilience, courage, and unwavering mental toughness. Take a moment to reflect on the stories of these remarkable individuals and identify aspects of their mental toughness that resonate with you.

Commit to a lifelong journey of learning and self-improvement. Be an inspiration for those around you, just as the icons in this exploration have been for you. Your journey toward mental toughness has the potential to motivate and uplift others facing their own challenges. By embracing these actions, you not only strengthen your own resilience but contribute to a collective culture of empowerment and growth.

OVER 10,000 PEOPLE HAVE ALREADY SUBSCRIBED. DID YOU TAKE YOUR CHANCE YET?

In general, around 50% of the people who start reading do not finish a book. You are the exception, and we are happy you took the time.

To honor this, we invite you to join our exclusive Wisdom University newsletter. You cannot find this subscription link anywhere else on the web but in our books!

Upon signing up, you'll receive two of our most popular bestselling books, highly acclaimed by readers like yourself. We sell copies of these books daily, but you will receive them as a gift. Additionally, you'll gain access to two transformative short sheets and enjoy complimentary access to all our upcoming e-books, completely free of charge!

This offer and our newsletter are free; you can unsubscribe anytime.

Here's everything you get:

✔ How To Start Mind Mapping eBook   ($9.99 Value)
✔ The Art Of Game Theory eBook   ($9.99 Value)
✔ Break Your Thinking Patterns Sheet   ($4.99 Value)
✔ Flex Your Wisdom Muscle Sheet   ($4.99 Value)
✔ All our upcoming eBooks   ($199.80* Value)

Total Value: $229.76

Go to wisdom-university.net for the offer!

(Or simply scan the code with your camera)

*If you download 20 of our books for free, this would equal a value of
199.80$

THE PEOPLE BEHIND WISDOM UNIVERSITY

Christoph Maurer, Founder and CEO

Christoph has always been a voracious reader with a writing talent. A bit less common, he has also been fascinated by business since he was a child. Consequently, after earning his degree in business management, he chose publishing as a full-time career. With his good friend of over 15 years, Michael, he founded Wisdom University. The company aims to build the most reader-centric original publishing house possible and become a household brand trusted by its dear readers. Practicing what he preaches, Christoph spends a considerable amount of time reading every day, deeply influenced by the examples set by Charlie Munger and Warren Buffet.

Michael Meisner, Founder and CEO

When Michael ventured into publishing books on Amazon, he discovered that his favorite topics - the intricacies of the human mind and behavior - were often tackled in a way that's too complex and unengaging. Thus, he dedicated himself to making his ideal a reality: books that effortlessly inform, entertain, and resonate with readers' everyday experiences, enabling them to enact enduring positive changes in their lives.

Together with like-minded people, this ideal became his passion and profession. Michael is in charge of steering the strategic direction and brand orientation of Wisdom University, as he continues to improve and extend his business.

Claire M. Umali, Publishing Manager

Collaborative work lies at the heart of crafting books, and keeping everyone on the same page is an essential task. Claire oversees all the stages of this collaboration, from researching to outlining and from writing to editing. In her free time, she writes online reviews and likes to bother her cats.

Kathleen Sperduti, Writer

Kathleen Sperduti is an experienced teacher, writer, and editor with a graduate degree in Education. Kathleen runs a parent association for families of children with disabilities, complex medical diagnoses, and learning needs. Her portfolio includes blog posts, magazine articles, e-books, and academic articles on a variety of topics. In her spare time, she enjoys language learning, traveling, reading, and knitting.

Andrew Speno, Content Editor

Andrew is a teacher, writer, and editor. He has published two historical nonfiction books for middle-grade readers, a biography of Eddie Rickenbacker and the story of the 1928 Bunion Derby ultra-marathon. He enjoys cooking, attending live theater, and playing the ancient game of go.

Sandra Agarrat, Language Editor

Sandra Wall Agarrat is an experienced freelance academic editor/proofreader, writer, and researcher. Sandra holds graduate degrees in Public Policy and International Relations. Her portfolio of projects includes books, dissertations, theses, scholarly articles, and grant proposals.

Jemarie Gumban, Publishing Assistant

Jemarie is in charge of thoroughly examining and evaluating the profiles and potential of the many aspiring writers for Wisdom University. With an academic background in Applied Linguistics and a meaningful experience as an industrial worker, she approaches her work with a discerning eye and fresh outlook. Guided by her unique perspective, Jemarie derives fulfillment from turning a writer's desire to create motivational literature into tangible reality.

Evangeline Obiedo, Publishing Assistant

Evangeline diligently supports our books' journey, from the writing stage to connecting with our readers. Her commitment to detail permeates her work, encompassing tasks such as initiating profile evaluations and ensuring seamless delivery of our newsletters. Her love for learning extends into the real world - she loves traveling and experiencing new places and cultures.

REFERENCES

1. From Setbacks To Success

1. Medarametla, A. (2021, February 12). LeBron James' Rise. *The Case Western Reserve Observer.* https://observer.case.edu/lebron-james-rise/
2. History-Biography. (n.d.). *Celebrity LeBron James.* History-Biography. https://history-biography.com/lebron-james/
3. Lyons, P. (2017). The 4 C's of Mental Toughness. *Ambition.* https://www.ambition.co.uk/blog/2017/02/the-4-cs-of-mental-toughness?
4. Malala Fund (n.d.). Malala's Story. *Malala Fund. https://malala.org/malalas-story*
5. Boren, C., (2022, September 15). A timeline of Roger Federer's glorious tennis career. *The Washington Post.* https://www.washingtonpost.com/sports/2022/09/15/roger-federer-career-timeline/
6. Hamilton, B. (n.d.). Biography: Bethany's Story. *Bethany.* https://bethanyhamilton.com/biography/
7. Piccotti, T. (2023, March 9). Oprah Winfrey. *Biography.* https://www.biography.com/movies-tv/oprah-winfrey
8. Lin, Y., Mutz, J., Clough, P. J., & Papageorgiou, K. A. (2017). Mental toughness and individual differences in learning, educational and work performance, psychological well-being, and personality: A systematic review. *Frontiers in psychology, 8,* 1345. https://doi.org/10.3389/fpsyg.2017.01345
9. Ruparel, N. (2020). Mental toughness: Promising new paradigms for the workplace. *Cogent Psychology, 7:1,* DOI: 10.1080/23311908.2020.1722354
10. Lee, M., & Kim, B. (2023). Effect of the Employees' Mental Toughness on Organizational Commitment and Job Satisfaction: Mediating Psychological Well-Being. *Administrative Sciences, 13*(5), 133. https://doi.org/10.3390/admsci13050133

2. The Mind's Influence

1. Dweck, C. S. (2006). *Mindset: The new psychology of success.* New York, NY: Random House.
2. Dweck, C. S. (2006). *Mindset: The new psychology of success.* New York, NY: Random House.

3. Schmitt, A., & Scheibe, S. (2022). Beliefs About the malleability of professional skills and abilities: Development and validation of a scale. *Journal of Career Assessment, 31(3)* 493-515. https://doi.org/10.1177/10690727221120367

4. Duckworth, A. L. (n.d.). *Angela Duckworth Grit Book.* Angela Duckworth. https://angeladuckworth.com/grit-book/

5. Duckworth, A. L., Quirk, A., Gallop, R., Hoyle, R. H., Kelly, D. R., & Matthews, M. D. (2019). Cognitive and noncognitive predictors of success. *Proceedings of the National Academy of Sciences, 116(47),* 23499-23504. https://doi.org/10.1073/pnas.1910510116

6. Meier, J.D. (n.d.). *Dealing with tough criticism — Think of it like a bucket of water, sand, and gold.* Sources of Insight. https://sourcesofinsight.com/a-bucket-of-criticism-water-sand-and-gold/

3. The Power Of Self-Reflection

1. Cleveland Clinic (n.d.). *Cognitive bias 101: What it is and how to overcome it.* Cleveland Clinic Health Essentials. https://health.clevelandclinic.org/cognitive-bias/

2. Cleveland Clinic (n.d.). *Cognitive bias 101: What it is and how to overcome it.* Cleveland Clinic Health Essentials. https://health.clevelandclinic.org/cognitive-bias/

3. Greenberger, G., & Padesky, C. (2016). *Mind over Mood, Second Edition.* The Guilford Press. https://www.guilford.com/books/Mind-Over-Mood/Greenberger-Padesky/9781462520428

4. Greenberger, G., & Padesky, C. (2016). *Mind over Mood, Second Edition.* The Guilford Press. https://www.guilford.com/books/Mind-Over-Mood/Greenberger-Padesky/9781462520428

5. Greenberger, G., & Padesky, C. (2016). *Mind over Mood, Second Edition.* The Guilford Press. https://www.guilford.com/books/Mind-Over-Mood/Greenberger-Padesky/9781462520428

6. Gomer, J., & Hill, J. (2015, July 14). *An essential guide to SWOT analysis.* Form Swift. http://mci.ei.columbia.edu/files/2012/12/An-Essential-Guide-to-SWOT-Analysis.pdf

4. Self-Confidence Is The Key

1. Wilson, R. (2023, March 9). *Self-Confidence vs. Self-Esteem.* Psychology Today. https://www.psychologytoday.com/intl/blog/the-main-ingredient/202303/self-confidence-vs-self-esteem

2. Carden, J., Jones, R. J., & Passmore, J. (2022). Defining self-awareness in the context of adult development: A systematic

literature review. *Journal of Management Education, 46*(1), 140-177. https://journals.sagepub.com/doi/10.1177/1052562921990065

3. Ackerman, C. (2018, July 9). *What is self-confidence (9+ proven ways to improve it).* Positive Psychology.

4. Wilson, R. (2023, March 9). *Self-Confidence vs. Self-Esteem.* Psychology Today. https://www.psychologytoday.com/intl/blog/the-main-ingredient/202303/self-confidence-vs-self-esteem

5. Wilson, R. (March 9, 2023). *Self-Confidence vs. Self-Esteem.* Psychology Today. https://www.psychologytoday.com/intl/blog/the-main-ingredient/202303/self-confidence-vs-self-esteem

6. Thierry, G. (2016). Neurolinguistic relativity: How language flexes human perception and cognition. *Language Learning, 66*(3), 690-713. https://onlinelibrary.wiley.com/doi/full/10.1111/lang.12186

7. Lupyan, G., Rahman, R. A., Boroditsky, L., & Clark, A. (2020). Effects of language on visual perception. *Trends in cognitive sciences, 24*(11), 930-944.https://doi.org/10.1016/j.tics.2020.08.005

8. Oaster, B. (2017). *Did you know your language changes how you see color?* Day Translations Blog. https://www.daytranslations.com/blog/language-changes-color/

9. Lupyan, G., Rahman, R. A., Boroditsky, L., & Clark, A. (2020). Effects of language on visual perception. *Trends in cognitive sciences, 24*(11), 930-944.https://doi.org/10.1016/j.tics.2020.08.005

10. Broditsky, L. (2011, February 1). *How language shapes thought: The languages we speak affect our perceptions of the world.* Scientific American. https://www.scientificamerican.com/article/how-language-shapes-thought/#:~:text=The%20answer%2C%20it%20turns%20out,causal%20role%20in%20shaping%20cognition.

11. American Psychological Association. (2020, February 1). *Building Your Resilience.* American Psychological Association. https://www.apa.org/topics/resilience/building-your-resilience

12. Cross, R., Dillon, K., & Greenberg, D. (2021, January 29). *The secret to building resilience.* Harvard Business Review. https://hbr.org/2021/01/the-secret-to-building-resilience#:~:text=In%20short%2C%20our%20resilience%20needs,%2Dto%2Dday%20life%20challenges.

13. Cross, R., Singer, J., & Dillon, K. (2021, May). *Resilience is a Team Sport.* Connected Commons. https://irc4hr.org/wp-content/uploads/2021/06/Resilience-is-a-Team-Sport.pdf

14. American Psychological Association. (2020, February 1). *Building Your Resilience.* American Psychological Association. https://www.apa.org/topics/resilience/building-your-resilience

15. Carnegie, D. (2017). *How to develop self-confidence and influence people by public speaking.* Simon and Schuster.

16. Ackerman, C. (2018, July 9). *What is self-confidence (9+ proven ways to improve it).* Positive Psychology. https://positivepsychology.com/self-confidence/

5. Setting And Aiming For The Right Targets

1. Smyth, A. P., Werner, K. M., Milyavskaya, M., Holding, A., & Koestner, R. (2020). Do mindful people set better goals? Investigating the relation between trait mindfulness, self-concordance, and goal progress. *Journal of Research in Personality, 88,* 104015. https://doi.org/10.1016/j.jrp.2020.104015 https://www.sciencedirect.com/science/article/abs/pii/S0092656620301045

2. Herrity, J. (2023, June 6). *Guide on how to write SMART goals (with examples).* Indeed. https://www.indeed.com/career-advice/career-development/how-to-write-smart-goals

3. Quantive. (n.d.). *What are OKRs? The ultimate guide to the objectives and key results framework.* Quantive. https://quantive.com/resources/articles/okr-meaning

4. Oregon State University. (n.d.). *WOOP goals.* Oregon State University. https://success.oregonstate.edu/learning/woop

5. Tracy, B. (n.d.). *The 80/20 rule. The Pareto Principle.* Brian Tracy International. https://www.briantracy.com/blog/personal-success/how-to-use-the-80-20-rule-pareto-principle/

6. Tracy, B. (n.d.). *The 80/20 rule. The Pareto Principle.* Brian Tracy International. https://www.briantracy.com/blog/personal-success/how-to-use-the-80-20-rule-pareto-principle/

7. Wilding, M. (November 9, 2020). *Why you need a personal mission statement.* Forbes. https://www.forbes.com/sites/melodywilding/2020/11/09/why-you-need-a-personal-mission-statement/?sh=7cc14cb359aa

8. Kristenson, S. (2022, October 7). *55 Personal mission statement examples for 2023.* Developing Good Habits. https://www.developgoodhabits.com/personal-mission-statement-examples/

9. Kristenson, S. (2022, October 7). *55 Personal mission statement examples for 2023.* Developing Good Habits. https://www.developgoodhabits.com/personal-mission-statement-examples/

6. Mastering Your Emotions

1. Serrat, O. (2017). Understanding and developing emotional intelligence. *Knowledge solutions: Tools, methods, and approaches to drive*

organizational performance, 329-339. https://doi.org/10.1007/978-981-10-0983-9_37

2. Serrat, O. (2017). Understanding and developing emotional intelligence. *Knowledge solutions: Tools, methods, and approaches to drive organizational performance*, 329-339. *https://doi.org/10.1007/978-981-10-0983-9_37*

3. World Health Organization. (2023, February 21). *Stress.* World Health Organization. https://www.who.int/news-room/questions-and-answers/item/stress

4. World Health Organization. (2023, February 21). *Stress.* World Health Organization. https://www.who.int/news-room/questions-and-answers/item/stress

5. Holman, D., Johnson, S., & O'Connor, E. (2018). Stress management interventions: Improving subjective psychological well-being in the workplace. In E. Diener, S. Oishi, & L. Tay (Eds.), *Handbook of well-being.* Salt Lake City, UT: DEF Publishers. DOI:nobascholar.com
https://nobascholar.com/chapters/44/download.pdf

6. Holman, D., Johnson, S., & O'Connor, E. (2018). Stress management interventions: Improving subjective psychological well-being in the workplace. In E. Diener, S. Oishi, & L. Tay (Eds.), *Handbook of well-being.* Salt Lake City, UT: DEF Publishers. DOI:nobascholar.com   https://nobascholar.com/chapters/44/download.pdf

7. Johns Hopkins Medicine. (n.d.). *Imagery.* Johns Hopkins Medicine. https://www.hopkinsmedicine.org/health/wellness-and-prevention/imagery#:~:text=Imagery%20(visualiza-tion)%20has%20harnessed%20the,help-ful%20it%20will%20likely%20be

8. Adams, A.J. (2009, December 3). *Seeing is believing: The power of visualization.* Psychology Today. https://www.psychologytoday.-com/ca/blog/flourish/200912/seeing-is-believing-the-power-visualization

9. Johns Hopkins Medicine. (n.d.). *Imagery.* Johns Hopkins Medicine. https://www.hopkinsmedicine.org/health/wellness-and-prevention/imagery#:~:text=Imagery%20(visualiza-tion)%20has%20harnessed%20the,help-ful%20it%20will%20likely%20be

7. The Influence Of Productive Habits

1. Merriam-Webster Dictionary (n.d.). *Habit.* Merriam-Webster Dictionary. https://www.merriam-webster.com/dictionary/habit
2. American Psychological Association (n.d.). *APA dictionary of psychology. Habit.* American Psychological Association. https://dictionary.apa.org/habit
3. Zahariades, D. (2020). *The mental toughness handbook: A step by step guide to facing life's challenges, managing negative emotions, and overcoming adversity with courage and poise.* Art of Productivity
4. Rubin, G. (2015). *Better than before: Mastering the habits of our everyday lives.* Hachette UK.
5. Duhigg, C. (2013). *The Power of Habit: Why we do what we do and how to change.* Random House.
6. Wood, W., & Neal, D. T. (2016). Healthy through habit: Interventions for initiating & maintaining health behavior change. Behavioral Science & Policy, 2(1), 71-83. https://behavioralpolicy.org/wp-content/uploads/2017/05/BSP_vol1is1_Wood.pdf
7. Wood, W., & Neal, D. T. (2016). Healthy through habit: Interventions for initiating & maintaining health behavior change. Behavioral Science & Policy, 2(1), 71-83. https://behavioralpolicy.org/wp-content/uploads/2017/05/BSP_vol1is1_Wood.pdf
8. The Washington Center for Cognitive Therapy (n.d.). *How to be better: The power of habit.* The Washington Center for Cognitive Therapy. https://washingtoncenterforcognitivetherapy.com/the-power-of-habit/
9. The Washington Center for Cognitive Therapy (n.d.). *How to be better: The power of habit.* The Washington Center for Cognitive Therapy. https://washingtoncenterforcognitivetherapy.com/the-power-of-habit/

8. Mindfulness Meditation

1. Paine, J. (n.d.). *11 wildly successful entrepreneurs who swear by daily meditation.* Inc. https://www.inc.com/james-paine/11-famous-entrepreneurs-who-meditate-daily.html
2. Marchand, W. R. (2014). Neural mechanisms of mindfulness and meditation: Evidence from neuroimaging studies. *World journal of radiology, 6*(7), 471-479. doi:10.4329/wjr.v6.i7.471 https://www.ncbi.nlm.nih.gov/pmc/articles/PMC4109098/
3. Matko, K., & Sedlmeier, P. (2019). What is meditation? Proposing an empirically derived classification system. *Frontiers in psychology, 10,*

2276. https://doi.org/10.3389/fpsyg.2019.02276 https://www.frontiersin.org/articles/10.3389/fpsyg.2019.02276/full

4. Van Vugt, M. K. (2015). Cognitive benefits of mindfulness meditation. *Handbook of mindfulness: Theory, research, and practice*, 190-207.

5. Van Vugt, M. K. (2015). Cognitive benefits of mindfulness meditation. *Handbook of mindfulness: Theory, research, and practice*, 190-207.

6. Marchand, W. R. (2014). Neural mechanisms of mindfulness and meditation: Evidence from neuroimaging studies. *World journal of radiology*, *6*(7), 471-479. doi:10.4329/wjr.v6.i7.471 https://www.ncbi.nlm.nih.gov/pmc/articles/PMC4109098/

7. Gelles, D. (n.d.). Well. How To Meditate. *The New York Times.* https://www.nytimes.com/guides/well/how-to-meditate

8. Matko, K., & Sedlmeier, P. (2019). What is meditation? Proposing an empirically derived classification system. *Frontiers in psychology*, *10*, 2276. https://doi.org/10.3389/fpsyg.2019.02276 https://www.frontiersin.org/articles/10.3389/fpsyg.2019.02276/full

9. American Psychological Association. (2019, October 30). *Mindfulness Meditation: A Research Proven Way to Reduce Stress.* American Psychological Association. https://www.apa.org/topics/mindfulness/meditation

10. Marchand, W. R. (2014). Neural mechanisms of mindfulness and meditation: Evidence from neuroimaging studies. *World journal of radiology*, *6*(7), 471-479. doi:10.4329/wjr.v6.i7.471 https://www.ncbi.nlm.nih.gov/pmc/articles/PMC4109098/

11. American Psychological Association. (2019, October 30). *Mindfulness Meditation: A Research Proven Way to Reduce Stress.* American Psychological Association. https://www.apa.org/topics/mindfulness/meditation

12. Marchand, W. R. (2014). Neural mechanisms of mindfulness and meditation: Evidence from neuroimaging studies. *World journal of radiology*, *6*(7), 471-479. doi:10.4329/wjr.v6.i7.471 https://www.ncbi.nlm.nih.gov/pmc/articles/PMC4109098/

13. Jha, A. P., Stanley, E. A., Kiyonaga, A., Wong, L., & Gelfand, L. (2010). Examining the protective effects of mindfulness training on working memory capacity and affective experience. *Emotion*, *10*(1), 54. https://doi.org/10.1037/a0018438

14. Van Vugt, M. K. (2015). Cognitive benefits of mindfulness meditation. *Handbook of mindfulness: Theory, research, and practice*, 190-207.

15. American Psychological Association. (2019, October 30). *Mindfulness Meditation: A Research Proven Way to Reduce Stress.* American

Psychological Association. https://www.apa.org/topics/mindfulness/meditation

16. Ackerman, C. (2017, January 18). *21 Mindfulness exercises and activities for adults (+ pdf).* Positive Psychology. https://positivepsychology.com/mindfulness-exercises-techniques-activities/

9. Embracing Life's Trials

1. Widely attributed to Scott Hamliton. See: Brainy Quote (n.d.). *Scott Hamilton Quotes.* Brainy Quote. https://www.brainyquote.com/quotes/scott_hamilton_259350

2. Hutyra, H. (2022, November 26). *6 types of adversity and how to overcome them.* Keepinspiring.me https://www.keepinspiring.me/6-kinds-of-adversity-and-how-to-overcome-them/

3. Hutyra, H. (2022, November 26). *6 types of adversity and how to overcome them.* Keepinspiring.me https://www.keepinspiring.me/6-kinds-of-adversity-and-how-to-overcome-them/

4. Seery, M. D., Holman, E. A., & Silver, R. C. (2010). Whatever does not kill us: Cumulative lifetime adversity, vulnerability, and resilience. *Journal of Personality and Social Psychology, 99*(6), 1025–1041. https://doi.org/10.1037/a0021344

5. Polizzi, C. P., & Lynn, S. J. (2021). Regulating emotionality to manage adversity: A systematic review of the relation between emotion regulation and psychological resilience. *Cognitive Therapy and Research*, 45, 577–597. https://doi.org/10.1007/s10608-020-10186-1

6. Perry, E. (2022, January 31*). 10 ways to overcome adversity and thrive during hard times.* BetterUp. https://www.betterup.com/blog/how-to-overcome-adversity

7. Macedo, T., Wilheim, L., Gonçalves, R., Coutinho, E. S. F., Vilete, L., Figueira, I., & Ventura, P. (2014). Building resilience for future adversity: a systematic review of interventions in non-clinical samples of adults. *BMC psychiatry, 14*, 1-8. https://link.springer.com/article/10.1186/s12888-014-0227-6

8. Macedo, T., Wilheim, L., Gonçalves, R., Coutinho, E. S. F., Vilete, L., Figueira, I., & Ventura, P. (2014). Building resilience for future adversity: a systematic review of interventions in non-clinical samples of adults. *BMC psychiatry, 14*, 1-8. https://link.springer.com/article/10.1186/s12888-014-0227-6

9. Polizzi, C. P., & Lynn, S. J. (2021). Regulating emotionality to manage adversity: A systematic review of the relation between emotion regulation and psychological resilience. *Cognitive Therapy and*

Research, 45, 577–597. https://doi.org/10.1007/s10608-020-10186-1

10. Polizzi, C. P., & Lynn, S. J. (2021). Regulating emotionality to manage adversity: A systematic review of the relation between emotion regulation and psychological resilience. *Cognitive Therapy and Research*, 45, 577–597. https://doi.org/10.1007/s10608-020-10186-1

Afterword

1. Widely attributed to Mark Victor Hansen. See: Haden, J. (n.d.). 50 Inspiring motivational quotes about mental toughness and willpower. Inc. https://www.inc.com/jeff-haden/50-inspiring-motivational-quotes-about-willpower-and-determination.html

1. That Psychological Edge

1. Byrne, C. (2024, January 8). *All about mental toughness: Definition, health effects, and how to get better at it.* Everyday Health. https://www.everydayhealth.com/emotional-health/mental-toughness/guide/

2. Liew, Guo Chen & Kuan, Garry & Chin, Ngien-Siong & Hashim, Hairul. (2019, July). Mental toughness in sport: Systematic review and future. *German Journal of Exercise and Sports Research*, 1 - 14. http://dx.doi.org/10.1007/s12662-019-00603-3

3. American Psychological Association. (2020, February 1). *Building your resilience.* https://www.apa.org/topics/resilience/building-your-resilience

4. Dweck, C. S. (2007). *Mindset: The New Psychology of Success.* Random House Publishing Group. https://www.penguinrandomhouse.com/books/44330/mindset-by-carol-s-dweck-phd/

5. Schmitt, A., & Scheibe, S. (2022). Beliefs About the malleability of professional skills and abilities: Development and validation of a scale. *Journal of Career Assessment, 31*(3) 493-515. https://doi.org/10.1177/10690727221120367

6. Lin, Y., Mutz, J., Clough, P. J., & Papageorgiou, K. A. (2017). Mental toughness and individual differences in learning, educational and work performance, psychological well-being, and personality: A systematic review. *Frontiers in Psychology, 8*, 1345. https://doi.org/10.3389%2Ffpsyg.2017.01345

2. Michael Jordan

1. Encyclopedia Britannica. (Updated 2023, November 9). *Michael Jordan*. Britannica. https://www.britannica.com/biography/Michael-Jordan

2. Chicago Bulls. (n.d.). *Michael Jordan*. Chicago Bulls History. Retrieved January 30, 2024, from https://history.bulls.com/players/michael-jordan/

3. Ganglani, N. (2023, March 26). "Get in the gym and work harder" - The advice Michael Jordan's mom gave him when he didn't make his high school varsity team. *Basketball Network*. https://www.basketballnetwork.net/old-school/advice-michael-jordans-mom-gave-him-when-he-didnt-make-high-school-team

4. Yun, D., Zhang, L., Qiu, Y., Schinke, R., & Liu, J. (2023). The usefulness of the useless: How ritualized behavior improves self-control under competition pressure. *Journal of Applied Sport Psychology*, 1-15. https://doi.org/10.1080/10413200.2023.2274465

5. Nelson, R. (2021, May 20). Inside Michael Jordan's game-day routine during 'The Last Dance.' *SLAM*. https://www.slamonline.com/the-magazine/michael-jordan-gameday-routine/

6. WTMG Team. (2023, February 26). What Michael Jordan said about mental skills. *Win the Mental Game*. https://www.winthementalgame.com/blog/michaeljordan

7. Contreras, C. (2023, July 21). How did NBA Legend Michael Jordan's father James die? *Oxygen True Crime*. https://www.oxygen.com/crime-news/how-did-michael-jordans-father-james-jordan-die#:~:text=But%20it%20was%20also%20a,October%201993%20to%20February%201994.

8. Medina, M. (Updated 2020, May 11). 'The Last Dance': Michael Jordan's retirement influenced by father's murder, not gambling. *USA Today*. https://www.usatoday.com/story/sports/nba/2020/05/11/the-last-dance-michael-jordan-retirement-father-murdered/3100158001/

9. Castrovince, A. (Updated 2022, January 2). The real story of MJ's baseball career. *MLB*. https://www.mlb.com/news/featured/michael-jordan-the-real-story-of-his-baseball-career

3. Asha Philip

1. Team GB. (n.d.). *Asha Philip*. Team GB. Retrieved January 30, 2024, from https://www.teamgb.com/athlete/asha-philip/IaYQSV714qgP7EHx3yjft

2. Bloom, B. (2019, March 1). Asha Philip: 'I was a double champion at two different sports, so surely I can do it at two different events.' *The Telegraph*. https://www.telegraph.co.uk/athletics/2019/03/01/asha-philip-double-champion-two-different-sports-surely-can/

3. BBC Ideas. (2020, September 8). *Mental toughness is the secret to success* [Video]. YouTube. https://www.youtube.com/watch?v=_iuPewWbp2U

4. British Athletics. (n.d.). *Asha Philip*. Retrieved January 30, 2024, from https://www.britishathletics.org.uk/athletes/asha-philip/

5. Ambition. (n.d.). *The 4 Cs of mental toughness*. Ambition. https://www.ambition.co.uk/blog/2017/02/the-4-cs-of-mental-toughness?source=google.ca

6. Dweck, C. S. (2007). *Mindset: The new psychology of success*. Random House Publishing Group. https://www.penguinrandomhouse.com/books/44330/mindset-by-carol-s-dweck-phd/

7. The National Lottery. (n.d.). Grassroots to glory - Asha Philip. Retrieved January 30, 2024, from https://www.lotterygoodcauses.org.uk/good-causes/grasroots-to-glory-asha-philip

4. David Goggins

1. Goggins, D. (2018). *Can't hurt me: Master your mind and defy the odds*. BookBaby. https://davidgoggins.com/book/

2. Mehta, V. (2022, October 1). The 2-word question that David Goggins uses to achieve the near impossible. *Medium*. https://medium.com/wholistique/the-2-word-question-that-david-goggins-uses-to-achieve-the-near-impossible-4854d2d2053d

3. Navy SEALS. (n.d.). *Hell week*. Retrieved January 30, 2024, from https://navyseals.com/nsw/hell-week-0/

4. Hargrave, M. (2023, September 28). *Kaizen: Understanding the Japanese business philosophy*. Investopedia. https://www.investopedia.com/terms/k/kaizen.asp

5. Parsons, M. (2023, March 1). 10 ideas of where to start Kaizen for self-improvement and powerful transformation. *Apollo Investing*. https://www.apolloadvisor.com/10-ideas-of-where-to-start-kaizen-for-self-improvement-and-powerful-transformation/

5. David Blaine

1. Blaine, D. (n.d.). *Frozen in time*. David Blaine. Retrieved January 30, 2024, from https://davidblaine.com/frozen-in-time/

2. Wolk, J. (200o, November 29). David Blaine unfreezes himself on ABC Tonight. *Entertainment Weekly*. https://ew.com/article/2000/11/29/david-blaine-unfreezes-himself-abc-tonight/

3. Shah, V. (2023, October 29). David Blaine: The magic of making the impossible, real. *Thought Economics*. https://thoughteconomics.com/interviewees/david-blaine/

4. Sharples, T. (2008, May 1). How David Blaine held his breath. *Time*. https://content.time.com/time/health/article/0,8599,1736834,00.html

5. American Psychological Association. (2017). *What is exposure therapy?* PTSD Clinical Practice Guideline. https://www.apa.org/ptsd-guideline/patients-and-families/exposure-therapy.pdf

6. Lin, Y., Callahan, C.P., & Moser, J.S. (2018). A mind full of self: Self-referential processing as a mechanism underlying the therapeutic effects of mindfulness training on internalizing disorders. *Neuroscience & Biobehavioral Reviews*, *92*, pp.172-186. https://doi.org/10.1016/j.neubiorev.2018.06.007

7. Walton, A. (2015, February 9). 7 Ways meditation can actually change the brain. *Forbes*. https://www.forbes.com/sites/alicegwalton/2015/02/09/7-ways-meditation-can-actually-change-the-brain/?sh=55f1aecf1465

8. Predoiu, R., Predoiu, A., Mitrache, G., Firanescu, M., Cosma, G., Dinută, G., & Bucuroiu, R. A. (2020). Visualisation techniques in sport - The mental road map for success. *Discobolul - Physical Education, Sport & Kinetotherapy Journal*, *59*(3). https://doi.org/10.35189/dpeskj.2020.59.3.4

9. Zaccaro, A., Piarulli, A., Laurino, M., Garbella, E., Menicucci, D., Neri, B., & Gemignani, A. (2018). How breath-control can change your life: A systematic review on psycho-physiological correlates of slow breathing. *Frontiers in Human Neuroscience*, *353*. https://doi.org/10.3389/fnhum.2018.00353

6. Oprah Winfrey

1. White, A. (2022, January 28). Gayle King reveals how an unexpected airport run-in led to Oprah's famous "You get a car!" giveaway. *The Hollywood Reporter*. https://www.hollywoodreporter.com/tv/tv-news/gayle-king-oprah-winfrey-show-car-giveaway-1235083395/

2. Fry, E. (Updated 2019, August 21). *A childhood biography of Oprah Winfrey.* Live About. https://www.liveabout.com/childhood-biography-of-oprah-winfrey-2535832

3. Capretto, L. (2016, January 2). The daring racism experiment that people still talk about 20 years later. *The Huffington Post*. https://www.huffpost.com/entry/jane-elliott-race-experiment-oprah-show_n_6396980

4. Batheja, A. (2018, January 10). The time Oprah Winfrey beefed with the Texas cattle industry. *The Texas Tribune*. https://www.texastribune.org/2018/01/10/time-oprah-winfrey-beefed-texas-cattle-industry/

5. Brown, D. (2017, August 15). How Oprah conquered her biggest failure (and how you can too). *Inc*. https://www.inc.com/damon-brown/how-oprah-conquered-her-biggest-failure-and-how-yo.html

6. Waxman, S. (1998, November 11). At the box office, 'Beloved' is a tough sell. *The Washington Post*. https://www.washingtonpost.com/archive/lifestyle/1998/11/11/at-the-box-office-beloved-is-a-tough-sell/f00fb51b-6bf6-4df7-9920-4c986f738715/

7. Van Meter, J. (2017, august 15). Oprah Winfrey is on a roll (again). *Vogue*. https://www.vogue.com/article/oprah-winfrey-vogue-september-issue-2017

8. Oprah Winfrey Charitable Foundation. (n.d.). *About us*. Retrieved January 30, 2024, from https://www.oprahfoundation.org/about-charity

9. The Associated Press. (1993, December 21). President Clinton signs the National Child Protection Act. *The New York Times National*. https://www.vachss.com/mission/president.html

10. Faster Capital. (n.d.). *The book clubs influence on diversity in literature*. Retrieved January 30, 2024, from https://fastercapital.com/topics/the-book-clubs-influence-on-diversity-in-literature.html

7. Serena Williams

1. Hess, L. (2022, August 9). The 9 greatest moments of Serena Williams's tennis career. *Vogue*. https://www.vogue.com/article/9-greatest-moments-serena-williams-tennis-career

2. Snyder Duke, K. (2020, September 9). Watch the moment 17-year-old Serena Williams won her first Grand Slam at the US Open. *POPSUGAR*. https://www.popsugar.com/fitness/serena-williams-wins-first-grand-slam-at-1999-us-open-47772423

3. Jiwani, R. (2023, May 2). *Serena Williams- tennis career statistics and facts*. Olympics. https://olympics.com/en/news/tennis-serena-williams-career-statistics-facts

4. Honderich, H. (2022, August 25). Serena Williams: How US Open victory of 1999 tells the story of what was to come. *BBC News.* https://www.bbc.com/sport/tennis/62661318

5. Encyclopedia Britannica. (Updated 2023, November 21). *Serena Williams.* Britannica. https://www.britannica.com/biography/Serena-Williams

6. Davis, S., Gopal, T. (2022, August 13*).* Serena Williams became the greatest tennis player of all-time even as she endured racist and sexist attacks in the media. *Business Insider.* https://www.insider.com/serena-williams-endured-racism-sexism-media-throughout-career-2022-8

7. Desmond-Harris, J. (Updated 2016, September 7). Serena Williams is constantly the target of disgusting racist and sexist attacks. *Vox.* https://www.insider.com/serena-williams-endured-racism-sexism-media-throughout-career-2022-8

8. Garcia, S., de Luca, A. (2022, September 2). Serena's game day hair. *The New York Times.* https://www.nytimes.com/interactive/2022/09/02/multimedia/serena-williams-tennis-hairstyles.html

9. S by Serena. (n.d.). *About us.* Retrieved January 30, 2024, from https://www.sbyserena.com/pages/about-us

10. Jimenez, J. (Updated 2022, September 3). In comebacks, Serena Williams showed 'you can never underestimate her.' *The New York Times.* https://www.nytimes.com/2022/08/29/sports/tennis/serena-williams-comebacks-us-open.html

11. Mitchell, R. (2022, July 15). *Angela Duckworth: The power of grit.* CFA Institute. https://blogs.cfainstitute.org/investor/2022/07/15/angela-duckworth-the-power-of-grit/

12. Serena's World. (n.d.). *Philanthropy.* Retrieved January 30, 2024, from https://www.serenawilliams.com/pages/philanthropy

13. UNICEF. (n.d.). *Serena Williams UNICEF Goodwill Ambassador since 2011.* Retrieved January 30, 2024, from https://www.unicef.org/goodwill-ambassadors/serena-williams

14. The Associated Press. (2023, November 17). Serena Williams and Ruby Bridges will be inducted into National Women's Hall of Fame. *NBC News. https://www.nbcnews.com/news/nbcblk/serena-williams-ruby-bridges-will-inducted-national-womens-hall-fame-rcna125677*

8. Vince Lombardi

1. CNBC. (Updated 2013, September 13). *Vince Lombardi - The number one speech.* https://www.cnbc.com/2008/06/13/vince-lombardi-the-number-one-speech.html

2. Pro Football Hall of Fame. (n.d.). *The ice bowl.* Retrieved January 30, 2024, from https://www.profootballhof.com/football-history/the-ice-bowl/

3. Puma, M. (----, September 13). Leader of men. *ESPN Classic.* Retrieved January 30, 2024, from http://www.espn.com/classic/Lombardi_Vince.html

4. Christl, C. (n.d.). *Vince Lombardi.* Packers. Retrieved January 30, 2024, from https://www.packers.com/history/hof/vince-lombardi#:~:text=No%20coach%20in%20National%20Foot-ball,%2D4%20regular%2Dseason%20record

5. Quantive. (n.d.). *What are OKRs? The ultimate guide to the objectives and key results framework.* Retrieved January 30, 2024, from https://quantive.com/resources/articles/okr-meaning

6. Radonić, M. (2017). OKR system as the reference for personal and organizational objectives. *From References to Originality, 28.* https://www.researchgate.net/profile/Milenko-Radonic-2/publication/346119547_OKR_System_as_the_Reference_-for_Personal_and_Oranizational_Objectives/links/5ff6e11aa6fdc-cdcb837d977/OKR-System-as-the-Reference-for-Personal-and-Oranizational-Objectives.pdf#page=27

7. Kristenson, S. (2022, October 7). 55 Personal mission statement examples for 2023. *Developing Good Habits.* https://www.developgoodhabits.com/personal-mission-statement-examples/

8. Trachtman, S. (Updated 2017, February 7). NFL head coaches with the best winning percentages of all time. *Yardbarker.* https://www.yardbarker.com/nfl/articles/nfl_head_coaches_with_the_best_winning_percentages_of_all_time/s1__22891306#slide_1

9. Barnett, C. (2019, January 1). Remember to K.I.S.S. when setting goals. *Medium.* https://cartermbarnett.medium.com/remember-to-k-i-s-s-when-setting-goals-98ca8571424d

9. Sara Blakely

1. SPANX. (n.d.). *About us.* Retrieved January 30, 2024, from https://spanx.com/pages/about-us

2. Evan, T. (2011, March 21). Sara Blakely on resilience. *Entrepreneur.* https://www.entrepreneur.com/leadership/sara-blakely-on-resilience/219367

3. O'Connor, C. (2015, June 10). From startup to mega-success: Lessons from Spanx's Sara Blakely, Ivanka Trump and more. *Forbes.* https://www.forbes.com/sites/clareoconnor/2015/06/10/from-

sexism-to-success-lessons-from-spanxs-sara-blakely-ivanka-trump-and-more/?sh=823bce87560c

4. Segal, G.Z. (2015, April 29). How billionaire Sara Blakely refused to let rejection stop her. *The Story Exchange*. https://thestoryexchange.org/sara-blakely-refused-fear-failure-stop/

5. Dyer, W. (1980). How to be a no-limit person. *Nightingale Conant*. https://www.nightingale.com/dyer-no-limit-person.html

6. Selva, J. (2018, March 8). *What is Albert Ellis's ABC model in CBT theory (Incl. pdf)*. Positive Psychology. https://positivepsychology.com/albert-ellis-abc-model-rebt-cbt/

7. Wirthman, L. (2013, August 19). Sara Blakely first woman billionaire to sign giving pledge. *Forbes*. https://www.forbes.com/sites/northwesternmutual/2013/08/19/sara-blakely-first-woman-billionaire-giving-it-away/?sh=9fa62e837368

8. SPANX by Sara Blakely Foundation. (n.d.). *Our journey*. Retrieved January 30, 2024, from https://www.spanxfoundation.com/journey/

10. Nelson Mandela

1. Nelson Mandela Foundation. (n.d.). *Trials and prisons chronology*. Retrieved January 30, 2024, from https://www.nelsonmandela.org/content/page/trials-and-prison-chronology#:https://www.nelsonmandela.org/content/page/trials-and-prison-chronology#:~:text=Nelson%20Mandela%20was%20arrested%20on,over%2027%20years%20in%20prison

2. Prince, A. (2020, June 16). 5 Lessons in reconciliation from Nelson Mandela. *LinkedIn*. https://www.linkedin.com/pulse/5-lessons-reconciliation-from-nelson-mandela-victor-prince/

3. Blakemore, E. (2020, July 17). *How Nelson Mandela fought apartheid-and why his work is not complete*. National Geographic. https://www.nationalgeographic.com/history/article/nelson-mandela-fought-apartheid-work-not-complete

4. Biography. (Updated 2022, January 7). *Nelson Mandela*. https://www.biography.com/political-figures/nelson-mandela

5. The Nobel Prize. (n.d.). *The Nobel Peace Prize 1993*. Retrieved January 30, 2024, from https://www.nobelprize.org/prizes/peace/1993/summary/

6. The Editors of Encyclopaedia Britannica. (Updated 2023, November 5). *Apartheid. Social policy*. Britannica. https://www.britannica.com/topic/apartheid

7. Nelson Mandela Foundation. (n.d.). *Biography of Nelson Mandela.* Retrieved January 30, 2024, from https://www.nelsonmandela.org/content/page/biography

8. Mandela, N. (1994). *Long walk to freedom.* Little, Brown & Company https://www.hachettebookgroup.com/titles/nelson-mandela/long-walk-to-freedom/9780759521049/?lens=little-brown

9. United Nations. (n.d.). *On freedom. "The struggle is my life." Press statement released on 26 June 1961.* United Nations Nelson Mandela International Day 18 July. Retrieved January 30, 2024, from https://www.un.org/en/events/mandeladay/struggle.shtml

10. McRae, M. (2018, July 17). *The story of Nelson Mandela.* The Canadian Museum of Human Rights. https://humanrights.ca/story/story-nelson-mandela

11. Myre, G. (2013, July 2). Nelson Mandela's prison adventures. *NPR.* https://www.npr.org/sections/parallels/2013/07/01/197674511/nelson-mandelas-prison-adventures

12. Gilmour, A. (n.d.). *The Nelson Mandela Rules: Protecting the rights of persons deprived of liberty.* United Nations, UN Chronicle. https://www.un.org/en/un-chronicle/nelson-mandela-rules-protecting-rights-persons-deprived-liberty#:~:text=At%20the%20Robben%20Island%20prison,and%20manual%20labour%20was%20discontinued.

13. Schaffner, A. K. (2023, June 1). *Understanding the circles of influence, concern, and control.* Positive Psychology. https://positivepsychology.com/circles-of-influence/

14. Evans, G. (2020, April 6). How Mandela stayed fit: From his 'matchbox' Soweto home to a prison cell. *The Conversation.* https://theconversation.com/how-mandela-stayed-fit-from-his-matchbox-soweto-home-to-a-prison-cell-135690

11. Malala Yousafzai

1. Yousafzai, M., Lamb, C. (2013). *The girl who stood up for education and was shot by the Taliban.* Little, Brown and Co. https://www.hachette-bookgroup.com/titles/malala-yousafzai/i-am-malala/9780316322409/?lens=little-brown

2. The Editors of Encyclopaedia Britannica. (Updated 2024, January 9). *Taliban.* Britannica. https://www.britannica.com/topic/Taliban

3. Al Jazeera. (2009, February 2). Pakistani Taliban rule Swat valley. https://www.aljazeera.com/news/2009/2/2/pakistani-taliban-rule-swat-valley

4. Brumsfeld, B. (Updated 2013, January 30). Malala's journey from near death to recovery. *CNN*. https://edition.cnn.com/2012/11/10/world/asia/pakistan-malala-one-month/index.html

5. Yousafzai, M. (2019, January 12). 'It felt as if we had landed on the moon': Malala Yousafzai on life in the UK. *The Guardian*. https://www.theguardian.com/books/2019/jan/12/it-felt-as-if-we-had-landed-on-the-moon-malala-yousafzai-on-life-in-the-uk

6. MasterClass. (Updated 2022, August 21). *Malala Yousafzai's story: A timeline of the activist's life.* https://www.masterclass.com/articles/malala-yousafzai-story

7. Zahra-Malik, M. (2013, October 11). *Malala, survivor of Taliban, resented in Pakistan hometown.* Reuters. https://www.reuters.com/article/uk-pakistan-malala/malala-survivor-of-taliban-resented-in-pakistan-hometown-idUKBRE99A07T20131011/

8. Mentzell Ryder, P. (2015, March). Beyond critique: Global activism and the case of Malala Yousafzai. *Literacy in Composition Studies Vol. 3*(1), 175-187. https://licsjournal.org/index.php/LiCS/issue/view/54/26

9. Watson Institute. (Updated 2023, March). *Costs of war. Pakistani Civilians.* Brown University. https://watson.brown.edu/costsofwar/costs/human/civilians/pakistani

DISCLAIMER

The information contained in this book and its components, is meant to serve as a comprehensive collection of strategies that the author of this book has done research about. Summaries, strategies, tips and tricks are only recommendations by the author, and reading this book will not guarantee that one's results will exactly mirror the author's results.

The author of this book has made all reasonable efforts to provide current and accurate information for the readers of this book. The author and their associates will not be held liable for any unintentional errors or omissions that may be found, and for damages arising from the use or misuse of the information presented in this book.

Readers should exercise their own judgment and discretion in interpreting and applying the information to their specific circumstances. This book is not intended to replace professional advice (especially medical advice, diagnosis, or treatment). Readers are encouraged to seek appropriate professional guidance for their individual needs.

The material in the book may include information by third parties. Third party materials comprise of opinions expressed by their owners. As such, the author of this book does not assume responsibility or liability for any third party material or opinions.

The publication of third party material does not constitute the author's guarantee of any information, products, services, or opinions contained within third party material. Use of third party material does not guarantee that your results will mirror our results. Publication of such third party material is simply a recommendation and expression of the author's own opinion of that material.

Whether because of the progression of the Internet, or the unforeseen changes in company policy and editorial submission guidelines, what is stated as fact at the time of this writing may become outdated or inapplicable later.

Wisdom University is committed to respecting copyright laws and intellectual property rights. We have taken reasonable measures to ensure that all quotes, diagrams, figures, images, tables, and other information used in this publication are either created by us, obtained with permission, or fall under fair use guidelines. However, if any copyright infringement has inadvertently occurred, please notify us promptly at wisdom-university@mail.net, providing sufficient details to identify the specific material in question. We will take immediate action to rectify the situation, which may include obtaining necessary permissions, making corrections, or removing the material in subsequent editions or reprints.

Made in the USA
Monee, IL
11 November 2024

69881890R00198